BERKSHIRE STUDIES
IN EUROPEAN HISTORY

Berkshire Studies

in European History

Under the editorship of
Richard A. Newhall and Sidney R. Packard

The Origins
of World War I
1871-1914

O the gondolets, the mandolins, the twangling of the lutes,
The girls all dressed in crinoline among the flowers and fruits—

The flowers all symbolical, the lily and the rose,
And how the sherry blossomed on the end of grandma's nose.

The maiden sighs and turns away, the maiden she relents,
Attracted by the glitter of a pile of five per cents.

They danced beneath the arbors, they strolled upon the grass,
O never aware, O never aware of what would come to pass.

THEODORE ROETHKE, *The Victorians*

The Origins
of World War I
1871-1914

Joachim Remak

Illustration on the cover are portraits of Czar Nicholas II (Granger
Collection), Wilhelm (The Bettmann Archive, Inc.) and Raymond
(Culver Pictures).

Poincaré's footnote's paper. The Americans to be printed by permission
© 1963, Stephen Ohizr, New York

HOLT, RINEHART and WINSTON
New York   Chicago   San Francisco   Atlanta   Dallas
Montreal   Toronto   London

Preface

Few events compare, in impact and terror, with World War I.
It destroyed two empires, that of the Habsburgs and that of the
Ottoman Sultans. It altered two others, that of the Hohenzol-
lerns and that of the Romanovs, beyond recognition. It created
a host of new nations in Europe and overseas. It gave birth to
Communist rule in Russia and provided the background for
Fascism in Italy and elsewhere. In its course, roughly twice as
many people were killed as in all the wars of the preceding two
centuries added together, the Napoleonic Wars and the American Civil War included. It also maimed, in body or spirit, many
of the survivors and laid the ground for an even more destructive World War II.

While the costs and consequences of World War I are matters
of fairly general agreement, its origins still are not. In the
immense literature on the causes of the war, a multitude of
explanations, many of them sharply at variance with each other,
have been advanced. But in this literature, for all the arguments
and the contradictions, four major topics, or groups of problems,
stand out. This book will deal with each of them in turn. The
first is the conduct of European diplomacy between 1871 and
1914. The second involves the problem of certain basic underlying sources of danger, such as the alliance system, imperialism,
and the role of public opinion. The third is the event that
provided the war's immediate cause, the assassination of Archduke Franz Ferdinand at Sarajevo. The fourth concerns the
conduct of European diplomacy in the five summer weeks that
passed between Sarajevo and the opening shot of the war.

In the writing of this book, several debts have been incurred,
which are gladly noted here. A number of publishers have kindly

agreed to the use of copyrighted material. They are listed in detail in the bibliographical essay which follows the last chapter, where some of the obligations owed to other historians who have written on the war's origins, the giants in particular—Fay, Schmitt, Sontag, Albertini—are indicated too. Various friends, colleagues, and students have contributed facts and ideas, notably Donald Balmer, John Crampton, and Nosratollah Rassekh at Lewis and Clark College; D. F. O'Brien at the Menlo Academy; F. Smith Fussner at Reed College; Wayne Vucinich at Stanford University; Geoffrey Smith at the University of California at Santa Barbara; Stephen Fischer-Galati at the University of Colorado; and Frederick A. Breier at the University of San Francisco. Above all, however, the author's gratitude goes to Norman Rich at Michigan State University for his criticisms and suggestions, hard in substance, kind in manner, that were based on his reading of the manuscript.

J. R.

University of California
Santa Barbara, California
April 1967

Contents

The Origins
of World War I
1871-1914

1 The Age of Bismarck: European Diplomacy 1871–1890

• *The Peace of Frankfurt and Some Consequences* The Franco-Prussian War of 1870–1871 opened a new age in European history. It meant the end of Napoleon III and the re-establishment of a French republic. It also meant the achievement of German unity under the leadership of a triumphant Prussia. France, by the terms of the Peace of Frankfurt that formally ended the war in May, 1871, agreed to pay an indemnity of five billion francs to the new German Empire. France also agreed to surrender the province of Alsace, and a substantial portion of Lorraine. And France was powerless to prevent what it had been able to obstruct for centuries past—the creation of a unified and strong German nation.

It was a diplomatic revolution, but a revolution, there was reason to hope, that would not be allowed to escape from the hands of its principal creator—Otto von Bismarck, Prime Minister of Prussia since 1862 and Chancellor of the German Empire during the first two decades of its existence from 1871 to 1890. Bismarck's aim, after Frankfurt, was peace. The Germans, he felt, had what they had set out to achieve, and what had so long eluded them, most notably in 1848—union and power. Germany henceforth should consolidate her gains and seek no new ones, not in Europe and not overseas. Her strength and fame were alarming enough to other nations as things stood. What Bismarck now wanted was calm; the new equilibrium of Europe ought not to be disturbed again. Bismarck's motives were not necessarily those of a philosophical opponent of force. They were, rather, the motives of a supremely astute politician who believed, rightly so, that the interests of Prussia-Germany, under the circumstances, happened to be best served by a long period of peace.

No matter what the motives were, the effects were largely happy ones. They would have been happier still, had not two problems remained that not all the skills of Bismarck could resolve. One was the problem of Alsace-Lorraine, the other that of the change in Europe's balance of power.

After Prussia's victory over Austria in 1866, Bismarck, in a scene heavy with emotion and barely suppressed violence, had fiercely argued against the victor's peace which the king and his generals had in mind. When the meeting was over, he collapsed with a crying spell; a while later, he contemplated suicide. But in the end, he had his way. The peace with Austria was a generous one, and the absence of any vindictive conditions left the future clear, as Bismarck had intended, for friendship with the former enemy.

There was no repetition of the scene after the Franco-Prussian War. The pressures for Prussia annexing Alsace-Lorraine were too strong, the grounds looked too valid. Prussia's king did not wish to be robbed of his triumph again. The generals argued that they needed the fortress of Metz in Lorraine to secure Germany against possible French attack. Public opinion demanded some concrete and, it seemed, entirely legitimate, fruits of victory; had not the name of the Alsatian capital more often been spelled Strassburg than Strasbourg?

Germany's river, Strassburg's *Dom*
Return them to their German home

wrote Heinrich von Treitschke, teaching history and
patriotism in Berlin.

Faced with this chorus of king, generals, professors, and
ordinary voters, Bismarck acquiesced. France, he consoled
himself, would not love Germany in any event, no matter
what the terms of the peace were. It wâs a specious argument, and the Chancellor was aware of it. For, plausible
though the reasons advanced for a victor's peace might
seem, all of them, in the end, proved to be very bad
indeed.

Bismarck's moral capital was immense; some plain
words on his part might have altered public opinion and
the king's as well. The Alsace might be German in language, but in sentiment it was not. Kellermann, Kléber,
Ney—the generals of the Revolution and of Napoleon,
those "bravest of the brave"—had opted for France just
as Steuben and the Muhlenbergs had opted for America.
1789 meant more than 1870; Paris was closer than Berlin.
And what held true for Alsace trebly held for Lorraine.
Before long, Treitschke was to become very angry with
Germany's new citizens. The Alsatians' desires were "mis-
guided"; they should be made to realize that they were
Germans, if need be by force. What of military necessity? Metz, said the chief of the Prussian general staff,
would be worth an army of 120,000 men. In a sense, it
was a brilliant estimate of the situation; after Frankfurt,
Germany possessed an ideal military frontier in the west.
In 1914, a very small German force would be able to hold
back a major French army there. In another sense, it was
a catastrophic misjudgment, since the establishment of
precisely this frontier would be one of the main reasons
why the two armies were advancing on each other in
1914. Too many Frenchmen would not resign themselves
to the loss of Alsace-Lorraine: "Always think of it, never

speak of it." In fact, speak of it; shroud in black the
statue of Strasbourg among the cities of France repre-
sented on the Place de la Concorde; shroud her in black
until 1871 might be undone.

Here, then, was one of the basic sources of discontent
after Frankfurt. The other was that Europe's balance of
power had materially changed. Of the five powers that
had been great before 1871, only England and Russia retained roughly their former places. Austria, once formidable, had become relatively weak, and so had France.
Conversely, Prussia—or rather Prussia-Germany now—
had risen to the rank of a major power. So, in some ways,
had a sixth—Italy, whose unification was complete now
that her leaders had taken advantage of the diversion of
the Franco-Prussian War to occupy Rome. Mainly, however, it was Germany's new position that was of concern.
Italy was a power largely by courtesy, power in the nineteenth century as in others being mainly measured in
guns rather than in Ghibertis, that is, by the ability to put
an effective army into the field in case of need.

Bismarck, feeling aware of both problems, took the approach that they were not insoluble. Nations can ultimately reconcile themselves to territorial losses. Shifts in
the balance of power do not automatically result in new
wars. His answer, over the period of his chancellorship,
was a threefold one. As for France: try to conciliate her.
Aid French ambitions elsewhere; perhaps Alsace could be
forgotten in time. "I want you to forgive Sedan, as after
1815 you came to forgive Waterloo," he said to the French
Ambassador. To this end, Bismarck was to encourage
French expansion into North Africa and China, support-
ing the French position in Tunis in the 1880s even at
the risk of antagonizing Italy, Germany's incipient ally.

As for the change in the balance of power: let the new
Germany speak and act softly; assure the world of her
pacific intentions. Thus Bismarck was to hold out as
long as he could against the acquisition of colonies.

When one of many visitors came to see him to urge that Germany, too, go exploring for ivory and ebony, Bismarck heard him out, and then said: "My map of Africa lies in Europe. Here is Russia, and there is France, and here in the middle are we. That is my map of Africa."

As for both the problem of France and of Europe's changed power structure: see to it that any French desire for revenge be kept in check by France's inability to find allies. Isolate her diplomatically, unless the alliance be with Germany—a possibility that, for all its remoteness, Bismarck did not exclude. But for the moment, keep France as friendless as Germany should be gregarious. International politics, he told a fellow diplomat, mainly reduced themselves to a simple formula: "In a world governed by five powers, try to be *à trois*."

• *The New Alliance System: The Three Emperors' League of 1873* The three Bismarck first joined together were Germany, Austria-Hungary, and Russia. A series of suitably festive state visits in 1872 involving William I, Francis Joseph, and Alexander II, followed by more prosaic and formal negotiations a year later, established the Three Emperors' League. Their governments would consult with one another on matters of mutual interest; and more importantly, they would maintain friendly neutrality—or even aid each other actively—in case any one of them should be attacked by another power.

The League made a fair amount of sense. There was Austria's need, particularly strong in view of her domestic problems, for a reconciliation with the Prussian enemy of 1866. There were the shades, particularly dear to the Russians, of the Holy Alliance, and tsarist hopes that the more conservative of the Big Five might once again make common cause against political innovation. There was, above all, Germany's desire to banish the specter of a two-front war. Should war ever come again, France, by herself, would not be a mortal threat; the combination of Russia and France would be. However, where the Three Emperors' League made less sense was in that of the three partners pledged to friendship, two, Russia and Austria, were in truth very much getting in each other's way in Southeastern Europe. Thus the League's first real test, the Congress of Berlin, nearly turned out to be its last.

• *The Decline of the Ottoman Empire, The Russo-Turkish War, and the Congress of Berlin of 1878* The events that led up to the Congress had some deep roots. The Turkish Empire, which had once reached from Hungary in the West to Persia in the East, from the Crimea in the North to Egypt in the South, was in a state of decline. The troubles that plagued it were many: old age, a corrupt and inefficient sultanate, a multiracial, multinational structure in a period when the fashion was for national independence.

The empire, while shrinking—the Crimea long ago had been lost to the Romanovs, Hungary to the Habsburgs—still struggled to maintain itself in the Near East and in the Balkans. Its principal nineteenth-century antagonists were of two sizes. There were the small Balkan nations, or those that meant to become nations—Greece, Albania, Bulgaria, Montenegro, Serbia, Rumania—who were openly anxious to be free of Ottoman rule, or to add to what independent territory they already held. Then there were the giants: Russia, Austria-Hungary, and now and then Great Britain and France. Their approach was less direct. Publicly, they spoke with sorrow about the woes of the supposedly sick man of Europe. Privately, they tended to hope for a speedy deterioration of his condition so that, in the case of Austria and Russia, they might fall heir to his position in the Balkans, and in that of Britain, France, and of Russia again, to those in the Near East.

Turkey's main chance for survival lay in the safety

offered by her ill-wishers' numbers. Had there been fewer presumptive heirs, the empire might well have been destroyed long before it actually was. As matters stood, Turkey possessed a certain amount of insurance in the inability of her adversaries to agree on a division of the spoils. Besides, when all was said and done, and this tended to be the British position in particular, enabling a weak Ottoman Empire to survive was preferable to allowing one of the rival powers of Europe to increase its strength at the Sultan's expense.

It was a precarious survival, however. More than once, Turkey had to put up with the intervention of the European powers in her internal affairs. The Greek War for Independence in the 1820s and the Crimean War three decades later provided some familiar examples. The 1870s now were to see one more.

In 1875, a revolt against Turkish rule broke out in the twin provinces of Bosnia and Herzegovina. This time, the usual pattern of unrest, rebellion, bloody suppression, and relative peace was broken. First, Serbia and Montenegro took up arms in defense of their Slavic brothers in Bosnia. Next, the revolt spread to Bulgaria, which had recently been granted some degree of autonomy within the Turkish Empire. The reasons for rebellion were much the same here as in Bosnia: economic discontent, a strong feeling of national consciousness, and hatred by the largely Christian population for the Moslem Turks. Finally, Russia decided, early in 1877, to join the battle against the Turks.

Russia's motives were a mixture of the old and the new. It had long been a desire of the Russians to see a weakened Ottoman Empire. What Russia had needed and wanted for centuries were the Dardanelles. The Russians could see no other way of having an assured access to the Mediterranean and thus to the world's commerce in times of peace, or of deploying their fleet with any true degree of effectiveness in times of war. "Would you deny me the keys to my house?" Alexander had asked Napoleon when they met at Tilsit to divide the world. Napoleon would; so would all the other statesmen of Europe. The aim remained.

The new but hardly contradictory motive was Pan-Slavism. It was Russia's historic mission, or so went the Pan-Slav argument, to protect and ultimately liberate the Slavs of Southeastern Europe presently living under foreign rule, Austrian or Turkish. All Slavs were brothers, and the term Slav was interpreted generously to include Poles, Bulgarians, Serbs, Slovenes, Czechs, Croats, Slovaks. Nor did all Pan-Slavs stop even there: some envisioned a truly Grand Federation of the East, to include Greece, (Orthodox in faith as was Russia) and above all, Constantinople. Constantinople would then receive its rightful name of Tsarigrad, the Imperial City, and union would reign between Moscow and Byzantium, between the Third Rome and the Second.

At times, the Russian government would frown on Pan-Slavism. Its program, obviously, was about as harmless as a forest fire. At other times, the government would smile on it. Pan-Slavism provided a useful diversion from tsardom's internal difficulties; it also had its uses in the pursuit of some very concrete Russian ambitions abroad.

During the early stages of the Bosnian and Bulgarian troubles, Alexander II had restrained the Pan-Slavs, but ultimately, the pressure for war proved too strong. The Pan-Slavs certainly had been right in one regard. The Turks were tired; the war was not a difficult one to win. Quite possibly, it was, as a foreign military observer put it, a battle between the one-eyed and the blind, but in a contest of this sort it is good to have one eye. A surprising Turkish stand at the Fortress of Plevna did slow the Russian advance and kept Russia from overrunning all of European Turkey, but even so, the Turks had little choice but to ask for peace and to accept it on Russia's terms.

The Treaty of San Stefano, which the two nations signed in March 1878, reflected the extent of Russia's triumph. Bulgaria was to become an autonomous principality, and a large principality it was to be, stretching from the Black Sea to the Adriatic. Rumania, Serbia, and Montenegro were to be independent in name as well as in fact, and the latter two were to increase their territory. Bosnia and Herzegovina were to become autonomous. To Russia directly went Rumanian Bessarabia, some territory in the Caucasus, and a vast indemnity. Turkey had largely been eliminated from Europe, and the continental holdings that remained had been split in two.

It was a victor's peace, and one which lacked all subtlety. The term "autonomy for Bulgaria" deceived no one, if only because San Stefano provided for a two-year Russian occupation of the principality. The Russians had acted with an astonishing disregard for anyone else's interests. Europe, quite predictably, took alarm.

The powers most immediately concerned were Great Britain and Austria-Hungary. England's role was the slightly more ambivalent of the two. Much of British public opinion tended to have a good deal of sympathy for the nations rising in rebellion against Turkey. William Gladstone, four times prime minister in the last quarter of the nineteenth century, published a celebrated pamphlet in 1876 on the "Bulgarian Horrors." In it, he damned the Turks for their cruelty and demanded what the Russians were in fact to force the Turks into granting: autonomy for the Balkan Christians. But Gladstone, Liberal and humanitarian, was not in office at the time. Benjamin Disraeli, Conservative and empire-minded, was; reasons of state mattered more to him than philanthropic impulses. It should be Britain's principal object, he wrote, "to keep the Russians out of Turkey, not to create an ideal existence for Turkish Xtians." Great Britain's interests in the Near East, Great Britain's concept of the balance of power, both precluded the acceptance of Russia's gains. Therefore, just prior to San Stefano, Disraeli had dispatched units of the British fleet to Constantinople; thus, he now was willing to go beyond naval demonstrations and contemplate war with Russia. The Balkan Christians might as well cease complaining; "autonomy for Ireland would be less absurd."

British opinion, at the spectacle of Russia's victories, came to side with Disraeli. The poor Bulgarians were forgotten; the Turks promoted from bloody oppressors of defenseless Christians to gallant fighters against the brutal Russians, England's ancient adversaries. It was the crisis that enriched the language with the word "jingoism":

> We don't want to fight,
> But by jingo if we do,
> We've got the men,
> We've got the ships,
> We've got the money too!

Were Britain to fight, at least one continental power might join her, Austria-Hungary. Austria's motives for opposing Russia's triumph were less ambitious than were Great Britain's. Vienna mainly wished to hold on to its possessions rather than add to the splendors of the empire. Austria's basic problems were not so dissimilar from Turkey's. It was a multiracial state, comprising within its borders at least a dozen different major nationalities and cultures, and nearly all of the religions known to man. Economically and historically, the empire made a very great deal of sense. Beside, it could be said of Austria what also (although with more reservations) could be said of Turkey: any institution that has lasted for some centuries and met its needs with some success deserves respect. Still, many of the nationalities that made up the empire took a less Burkean view of things. In varying degrees, they were feeling dissatisfied with their role in the monarchy, resenting what they considered to be excessive German and Magyar domination. In the case of the Magyars, these grievances could be only too well documented: Budapest's nationality policy was distinguished neither by its generosity nor by its tolerance. Vienna's record was far better, as good as that of any pluralistic empire, Rome included. But the restiveness remained, particularly among the monarchy's Slavic population. The men in charge of Austrian policy, in consequence, were aghast at San Stefano. What were they to make of Russia's broken word? Bosnia and Herzegovina, the tsar had promised before he was sure of victory, were to go to Austria. How was Austria-Hungary to live with Russia's suddenly overwhelming presence in the Balkans?

The Bosnian question was at the core of it. Again, it was not so much that Austria coveted new territory. The monarchy was having enough to worry about with what it already encompassed. It was rather that Vienna could visualize what would happen if the newly autonomous region should one day join Serbia. The greater Serbian kingdom thus created would be a frighteningly attractive magnet to the empire's South Slav citizens. Perhaps Austria, too, should give battle to undo San Stefano—without any bellicose lyrics, sadly rather, as became the Austrian mood—but battle nonetheless.

The man who in the end was instrumental in keeping anyone from fighting was Bismarck. Peace was his platform; no Balkan troubles would dislodge him from it. In the summer of 1878, the powers agreed to meet at Berlin, to reconsider, under Bismarck's chairmanship, the provisions of San Stefano. The Congress, to the shock of the Russians, all but demolished the treaty. Not that everything went wrong for the Russians at the Congress of Berlin. The independence of Serbia and Montenegro was confirmed, although their borders were slightly redrawn. Confirmed, too, were most of Russia's direct gains, notably Kars, Batum, and Bessarabia. However, the principality of Bulgaria was deprived of its access to the Aegean and reduced to one-third the size envisaged at San Stefano. Moreover, Russia's gains were balanced by compensating the other powers at Turkey's expense. Britain received Cyprus. The French received clearance to move from Algeria into Tunis. The Austrians received Bosnia and Herzegovina, nominally, to "occupy and administer"; actually, there was no need to spell out how many tenths of the law comprised possession.

Only the Germans demanded, and the Italians received, nothing. Germany was satisfied to play the role of "honest broker"; here was as good an opportunity as any to display the new Reich's political moderation. As for the other newly unified nation, enforced moderation seemed the essence of wisdom. The Italians, said Bismarck, had such a large appetite and such poor teeth.

True unhappiness over the results of the Congress was reserved, however, to the Russians and to the Balkan nations. The Russians felt deserted by the Germans at Berlin—where was the support they should be receiving from their ally of the Three Emperors' League? Equally bitter was the sentiment in the Balkans. For the most part, independence or autonomy stood confirmed, but the new borders seemed to have been drawn with considerable disregard for ethnic realities and national ambitions. The Rumanians resented the loss of Bessarabia. The Greeks felt that their aspirations had not received a proper hearing. The Serbians mourned for the loss of Bosnia and Herzegovina. The Bulgarians would not reconcile themselves to the disappearance of the mirage of a Greater Bulgaria conjured up at San Stefano.

It was easy enough to counter these objections. Russia, after all, had brought her Berlin defeat upon herself by her greed at San Stefano. The powers of Europe had valid cause for being more interested in preventing the diplomatic revolution that would have resulted from the destruction of European Turkey according to the Russian pattern than in establishing ethnic justice in South-eastern Europe. Besides, not all the wisdom of Solomon could have defined the meaning of justice in this case; the man did not exist who could have drawn indisputably equitable borders in this part of the world. Greece, Rumania, and Serbia certainly had not been noticeably happier with San Stefano than they were with Berlin.

All such arguments, however, did not change the fact that taken together, the Balkan Wars, San Stefano, and Berlin provided two of World War I's long-range causes. One was that the unresolved discontents of Southeastern Europe were to be at the root of several subsequent Balkan crises and perhaps even of Sarajevo. The other was the ominous estrangement between Russia and Germany.

• *The Dual Alliance of 1879* Publicly, Bismarck had been charm itself at the Congress of Berlin. Privately, he was seething. For three years now, ever since the beginning of the Balkan imbroglio, he had been doing his utmost to prevent a break between Austria and Russia. He had no wish to take sides between his allies. Never cut the wire to St. Petersburg, was his maxim. Never cut the wire to Vienna either.

Berlin had ended that. He had labored hard at the Congress to find a fair compromise. He had labored in vain. The Three Emperors' League was dead. The Russians, ready as always to indulge their sense of grievance, were fuming at him, from tsar on down to inspired press.

Forced to make the next move now, Bismarck replaced the Three Emperors' League with a bipartite treaty with Austria, the Dual Alliance of 1879. Designed to last for an initial period of five years, it was renewed periodically, and thus did not expire until the two imperial regimes signing it did, in 1918. It was a defensive alliance under whose terms the signatories agreed to come to each other's aid, should Russia attack either country. Should a coun-

try other than Russia be the aggressor, the treaty partner
would maintain a position of benevolent neutrality, unless Russia should join the war, in which case armed
assistance again was mandatory.

The Dual Alliance has received strong criticism. Bismarck, his critics charged, had tied the fate of a vigorous
Germany to that of the troubled Habsburg monarchy.
He also, by opting for Austria, was forcing the Russians to
seek an alliance elsewhere, specifically, with France.

Bismarck took both of these objections into account.
As for tying Germany's fate to that of Austria, the Germans would plainly have to be on guard here. But who,
after all, was really tied to whom? Every alliance, said
Bismarck, had a horse and a rider, and in this one, Germany should easily be in the saddle. What the rider
must do was remain alert and restrain the horse. Germany ought never to encourage, he wrote the German
Ambassador at Vienna in a typical instruction of the mid-
eighties, "the temptations, to which the Austrians are
prone, to exploit the situation in order to use the armed
forces of Germany for the benefit of Hungarian and
Catholic ambitions in the Balkans." The term "defensive" in the alliance would have to mean just that. If
Austria should ever be a victim of Russian attack, German aid would freely be given, "but an *attack* on Russia
is something we will not engage in, nor will we, in case
Austria should undertake it, consider the alliance to be
operative. . . . For us, Balkan questions can never be a
motive for war."

But what of the offense that Russia might take at any
sort of special and exclusive Hohenzollern-Habsburg
partnership? Here, too, Bismarck was able to think several
moves ahead. He did not believe that Russia could or
would turn to the West. Ideologically and diplomatically,
too much divided the land of the tsars from Britain and
France. He did believe that Russia, when faced with a
firm commitment between Austria and Germany, and

thus with the prospect of diplomatic isolation, would trade resentment for realism. In diplomacy as in politics, there can be no permanent enmities.

• *The Three Emperors' League Renewed, 1881* His calculation proved to be correct. The Dual Alliance had hardly been signed when the Russians began to suggest a Russo-German alliance. Negotiations were slow, for Bismarck wished Austria to be included. He was to have his way. In 1881, Russia, Germany, and Austria formally signed an agreement reviving the Three Emperors' League. The treaty's scope was broader than that of its predecessor. The contracting parties agreed, with no defensive clause this time, that if any one of them should "find itself at war" with a fourth power, the other two would remain neutral. This went far to relieve Germany's dread of a two-front war against both Russia and France. It also helped to alleviate Russia's fear of an Austro-British military coalition against her that had been such a distinct possibility in 1878. In one respect, however, the new Three Emperors' League was narrower in scope. It contained a major qualification concerning the applicability of its provisions in that region of Europe where Austro-Russian interests were most at variance. The promise of neutrality, read the treaty, was to apply in case of war against Turkey only on condition that the three signatories first agreed on "the results of this war" or, more plainly put, on a division of the spoils.

One Turkish spoil already distributed in 1881 was Bosnia-Herzegovina. Austria, under the terms of the treaty, received the right to annex the two provinces "at whatever moment she shall deem opportune." Russia, in return, received assurances that the Straits were to remain closed to warships of all nations; Russia was to be secure from naval attacks from the Black Sea. This was a matter of particular concern to the Russians, who had done little to rebuild the Black Sea fleet destroyed in the Crimean

War and thus had good reason to fear a British fleet sailing through the Straits, guns pointed at Odessa or Sevastapol.

It was a good treaty in all. As seen from Russia and Austria, some very specific gains could be noted—the Bosnian concession and the Black Sea clause, and beyond that, the implicit establishment of an armistice in the Balkans. Obviously, much would depend on the spirit in which the treaty would be observed, but chances were fair that the Balkan truce might turn into genuine peace. As seen from Bismarck's chancellery, the gains were less direct but even more pleasing: Germany was *à trois* again, France *tout seul*.

• *The Triple Alliance of 1882*   In fact, the Germans were to gain one more ally. In 1882, attracted by power and offended by France, Italy asked to join the Austro-German Dual Alliance. The Italians, eager for empire, had for some time had their eyes on Tunis, but the French hand was quicker than the Italian eye. In 1881, the French, moving from Algeria, established a Tunisian protectorate. The Italians were outraged, the more so since they were unable to offer any effective resistance to France. The consequence was a search for allies, even for so unlikely an associate as Austria, whose popularity was no greater than that of France, since the Trentino and Trieste —"unredeemed Italy"—were still in Habsburg hands.

Bismarck's enthusiasm was muted. He feared that once the Austrians made their peace with Rome and felt secure to the southwest, they might again become hard to handle in their Balkan conflicts with Russia. But in the end, he agreed to a defensive alliance. Its most specific provisions dealt with France. Should France, "without direct provocation," attack Italy, Austria and Germany would come to Italy's aid. Should France attack Germany, Italy, in turn, would provide military support to her ally.

Of the five great European powers with which he had

to reckon, Bismarck now was on good terms with one, Great Britain, (no part of the Triple Alliance, stated a supplementary declaration, should "in any case be regarded as directed against England") and formally allied with three others, Italy, Russia, and Austria. If only he could keep his friends from coming to blows with each other, he would have no cause to fear his enemy. But controlling all of his friends all of the time proved to be beyond even his powers. In 1885, a new Balkan crisis unfolded which once more forced Bismarck into the role he was least inclined to play, that of arbiter between Russia and Austria.

• *The Bulgarian Crisis and the End of the Three Emperors' League, 1885–1887*   The Balkan nation that had lost more than any other at the Congress of Berlin had been Bulgaria. In 1885, the Bulgarians saw an opportunity to recover much of what they had lost seven years earlier. A revolt had broken out in Eastern Rumelia, a region Bulgarian in population and sympathy. It had, accordingly, been made a part of the Greater Bulgaria created at San Stefano, but the Congress of Berlin, while granting it autonomy, had returned it to Turkish suzerainty. The Bulgarians, understandably, decided to support the new rebellion, which had the exchange of autonomy for union with Sofia as its aim.

Bulgaria faced two major obstacles. This time, there was no Russian aid; the new nation had shown itself far too independent in spirit and action for the Tsar's taste. There also was Serbia's hostility. Belgrade was not sure that it could live with a too triumphant Bulgaria; it also sensed that this might be the time to settle the fate of Macedonia, that ancient and bitter issue among Serbia, Greece, and Bulgaria.

The Serbians decided on war. Peaceful habits would have become them more. With speed and skill, they were routed by the Bulgarians. Only Serbia's alliance with Austria, concluded in 1881, saved her from utter disaster.

Bulgaria's triumph was too great for Russia's comfort. The tsar now threatened to occupy Bulgaria and to put a more pliant ruler on her throne. This move brought Austria onto the scene again. As long as it had been a fight between Serbians and Bulgarians and the principal object was Eastern Rumelia, the Austrians could afford to be anti-Bulgarian. Now that Russian intervention threatened, they no longer could. Self-defense seemed to require a stand in favor of Bulgaria; Pan-Slavism had to be stopped somewhere.

The outcome was a diplomatic victory for the Austrians. Ably assisted by Great Britain—where the prospect of a Russian-dominated Balkans was no more attractive now than it had been at the time of Berlin—Austria prevented the Russian move. The Russians were infuriated, directing their anger at friend and foe alike. In the face of the many appeals that came to him from Vienna and St. Petersburg in the course of the crisis, Bismarck had tried hard to remain neutral, siding, if anything, with Russia at first, but too concerned, on the other hand, with the fear of losing his Austrian ally to give the Russians the unquestioning support they demanded as their right. In consequence, Russia now despised the Germans nearly as much as she did the Austrians, and in 1887, as the Bulgarian crisis was ending, so, too, was the Three Emperors' League.

• *From the Reinsurance Treaty to the Fall of Bismarck, 1887–1890* The League had been signed for a period of as many years as there were emperors in it. In 1884, when it first came up for renewal, the Russians were happy to sign again. In 1887 they were not. But their respect for realities was strong enough to make them propose a bipartite agreement to Germany. It was not the kind of treaty Bismarck would have chosen, but it was better than none. Hence, in 1887, he signed what came to be known as the Reinsurance Treaty with Russia. If either power should find itself at war, the other would maintain a benevolent neutrality. The only exception was to be aggressive war. Should Russia attack Austria, or should Germany attack France, the treaty partner would have full freedom of action.

The Russians received what looked like a great deal for having insured the Germans against a two-front war. Germany recognized Russia's preponderant influence in Bulgaria; reaffirmed the principle of the closure of the Straits; and, better than that, promised moral and diplomatic support for any measures the tsar might take to control the key of his Empire.

Bismarck seemed to have given far more than he received. Seemed to have, for in truth Russia's gains were largely paper gains. In perhaps the most intricate series of diplomatic maneuvers of his career, Bismarck was seeing to that. Even before the formal completion of the Reinsurance Treaty, he had been party to bringing about a Mediterranean Agreement between Great Britain, Austria, and Italy, in which the three powers undertook to maintain the status quo in the Balkans, the Near East, and North Africa. In this way his promises to Russia were effectively neutralized, for what he had in truth granted to the Russians was something that he knew the British and Austrians could be relied on to withhold from them. Next, he allowed the terms of his various secret agreements to leak out. To impose some sensible caution on the Russians in the Balkans, he let them know about the Dual Alliance with Austria. So that they might have no doubt about the strength of the coalition that would face them should they try to pocket the house key, he let them know about the Mediterranean Agreement as well. The Austrians, in their turn, had the Reinsurance Treaty brought to their attention; it would be a good reminder that German aid was not automatic. Finally he let the French learn about both the Triple Alliance and the Mediterranean Agreement; it would do them no harm to realize that the world contained potential enemies other than the occupiers of Alsace.

While these maneuvers may have been several shades too complex and too subtle, and leavened with rather more than the ordinary amount of diplomatic duplicity, what needs to be said for them is that they worked, that they served Bismarck's overriding motive of maintaining peace. The multiplicity of alliances did make for caution; Vienna as well as St. Petersburg found it politic to restrain their ambitions. How well the system would work without its original engineer was a different question. The answer would come all too soon. In 1890, Bismarck had to step down as chancellor. Ostensibly, policy differences between him and the new Emperor, William II, played a major part in his dismissal. Actually, the principal reason, and for once we should have some sympathy for William II, was that the young monarch found it understandably difficult to get along with a national monument for a chancellor. Still, the pilot was gone; Europe would not be the same again.

Bismarck's achievement, as we look back on the two decades of his chancellorship, is as astonishing as ever. He had voluntarily restrained Germany's quest for power. The sky was the fool's limit, not his. He had built an alliance system that left France without allies, and Germany with as many as any one power could manage. The diplomatic alignment of 1914 was in a future more remote than the quantum theory. Russia was still allied to Germany, Austria was ready to fight in the defense of Serbia, and England and Russia invariably found themselves on opposite sides. Of the conflicts that remained, some seemed perfectly capable of pacific solution, and those that perhaps were not, still did not seem worth the cost of a general war. As much as any one man, Bismarck had helped to create the late nineteenth-century mood of Europe, which appeared to take it for granted that war was an aberration, and that peace was man's natural estate.

2 Triple Alliance and Triple Entente: European Diplomacy 1890–1914

• *The Initiative Passes: The Re-emergence of France*

That Bismarck's successors would not be his equals might have been expected; that quite so much would divide them from him was another matter. The Kaiser by no means lacked intelligence, but he used it badly. For all his occasional charm and judgment, he was unstable, impulsive, incapable of sustained effort, uncertain of his aims, and given to bluster. His public speeches had a way of disconcerting his friends and delighting his enemies. They abounded with talk of might and "shining armor"; of a German future that lay on the water; of "days of splendor" toward which he was leading his nation, although along that road to glory there would then be more than one instance of "my and my people's exhausted patience." They contained supreme imbecilities such as his claims to divine right—he was "the instrument of the Lord," who would go his way "without regard for daily opinions and intentions"—or his famous exhortation to the German troops leaving for China after the Boxer rebellion:

You must know, my men, that you are about to meet a crafty, well-armed, cruel foe! Meet him and beat him! Give no quarter! Take no prisoners! Let his life be forfeit if he falls into your hands! Just as, a thousand years ago, the Huns under their king Attila made a name for themselves which makes their power resound in legend and fable to this very day, so may you affirm the German name in China in such a manner that never again will a Chinese dare as much as look askance at a German!

Not all his speeches were this outrageous, nor did the spirit really match the bluster. Nevertheless, there was now no Bismarck to counsel or restrain him. In part, this was the Emperor's own fault: flattery carried more weight with William II than talent. However, one need not exaggerate that point; the men who held office under him were not incompetents or fools, and although a French observer would call the man who followed Bismarck into the foreign ministry the *ministre étranger aux affaires*, this was moderately funny but untrue. He as well as his colleagues knew their subject well enough; all they lacked was genius, and later, courage. And they were aware of this. "What kind of jackass will dare to be Bismarck's successor," General von Caprivi once asked a friend. When, not much later, William II asked Caprivi to succeed Bismarck as chancellor, the general's initial reaction was to reply that Bismarck dead and carried in front of the Emperor like the Cid would be of more use to the country than he, Caprivi, alive. Having accepted the office for all his misgivings, it was Caprivi who also coined the famous description of Bismarck as the man who alone could keep five glass balls in the air at the same time. There was an element of truth in the image, nor is it easy not to sympathize with Caprivi. The analogy of the five balls certainly turned into a comfortable cliché until a young Swiss historian, Leonhard von Muralt, recently suggested that if it were true, Caprivi had no right to remain in office. The number of balls, after all, had not decreased just because Caprivi said that no one but Bismarck could juggle them.

Another power was now willing to try some difficult juggling, the power that had been in apparent eclipse during the past two decades—France. What Germany most notably lacked in the quarter century before 1914, France possessed—diplomatic genius. No one person would dominate the scene in Paris as Bismarck had in Berlin, but amóng an abundance of talent, four men at least stand out: Delcassé, Poincaré, and Paul and Jules Cambon.

Théophile Delcassé, long a parliamentary deputy, served as colonial secretary in the early 1890s, as foreign minister from 1898 to 1905, then as secretary of the navy, and, after 1914, as foreign minister again. His admirers' epithet, "France's answer to Bismarck," was far from wrong. He could move among very different allies with ease. He could tell the essential from the ephemeral. He could make some clear choices where indecision while pleasant, was folly; it was Delcassé who faced the fact that France could not afford the luxury of forever living at cross-purposes with both Britain and Germany and who, at the risk of antagonizing considerable parts of French public opinion, set to turning one of the two into a friend.

He was splendidly supported by the two Cambon brothers. Paul Cambon, during the period that Delcassé was foreign minister and for some years thereafter, was ambassador to Great Britain; Jules Cambon, after holding office as governor-general of Algeria, served as ambassador in Washington, Madrid, and Berlin. Their reports are models of lucidity. Their approach to diplomacy brings to mind Bismarck's more celebrated than heeded dictum about politics as the art of the possible; it was Paul Cambon who would say, apropos of his recommendation for reaching a *rapprochement* with Russia: "If you cannot have what you like, you must like what you have." He would have generous opportunity to work toward that end, for one other aspect of French foreign policy of the period that deserves special note was its continuity. Cabinets came and went, but foreign ministers and ambassadors remained. Delcassé served throughout the lives of six subsequent ministries; Paul Cambon would represent France at the Court of Saint James for twenty-two years.

Finally (or rather finally in this select list only) there was Raymond Poincaré, senator, minister of finance, premier, and, in 1913, President of the Republic. A native of Lorraine, Poincaré was as passionate a Frenchman and republican as Bismarck had been a Prussian and a monarchist. He was a man of shrewdness, probity, great energy, and that particularly French combination of rationalism and conservatism; some writers have seen him as the personification of all that has been best in bourgeois France. He was intent on building up French strength against Germany, not so much because he wished for a war of revenge as because he felt that William's Germany was as likely as not to start a war, and that France needed to be prepared.

In all, the period would provide a striking example of the importance of individual talent in the conduct of the affairs of state. Militarily, demographically, and economically, France was hardly any more powerful in the quarter century prior to 1914 than in the years from 1871–1890; Germany was scarcely any less so. Yet the initiative was slipping from German hands and it was in those of France that it largely came to rest. If the diplomatic capital of Europe, for decades, had been Berlin, it now was Paris again, and it was neither guns nor the gross national product that caused the shift.

• *The Road to the Franco-Russian Alliance, 1890–1894*
French intelligence was aided by German error. Within

days of Bismarck's fall, the foreign ministry persuaded the Kaiser not to renew the Reinsurance Treaty with Russia, which, unless signed again, was due to expire that summer. The Russians pleaded with Berlin, but the German decision stood. The treaty was allowed to lapse.

One should restrain any easy criticism of the German attitude in 1890. There had been something bordering on the miraculous in Bismarck's performance. Remaining allied to both Austria and Russia was a feat that struck his successors as only slightly less difficult than squaring the circle. The magician was gone now. It might be better to devise a foreign policy that ordinary mortals could manage. What profit had there really been in finding oneself in the middle of every Austro-Russian argument?

Besides, the cancellation of the Reinsurance Treaty might well result in attracting a new and rather more desirable ally in the West. The old Chancellor had for some time been trying to draw Great Britain into his alliance system. Now that Germany could no longer be suspected of making common cause with Britain's enemy, Russia, the time seemed propitious to resume the effort. British power was rather more formidable than Russia's in any event, and feelings of kinship a good deal stronger.

There ensued a number of friendly gestures toward Britain. 1890 saw the conclusion of an Anglo-German treaty in which the Germans made some major concessions to the British in East Africa in return for having the tiny island of Heligoland in the North Sea ceded to them. The next year, a grand state and family visit took place as William II traveled to London to pay his respects to his aged grandmother, Queen Victoria.

No matter how sincere those gestures or how valid the motives, the result was a double failure. The Germans had lost one ally without gaining another. The British were not persuaded to join the Triple Alliance; they were chary of cousins bearing gifts. The Russians, on the other hand, faced by the new German coolness toward them, felt humiliated and worried. The old pattern lay broken. So far, after each crisis, they had exploited the facility with which they took diplomatic offense to demand a higher price for returning to their German alliance. This time, Berlin apparently did not wish them to return, even at lowered rates. The Russians were ready to listen to some other offer.

That other offer came from France. Many people in Europe—some members of the German foreign ministry included—had thought that an alliance between France and Russia was wholly out of the question. A political chasm divided them: France, republican and devoted to the ideals of the Great Revolution of 1789; Russia, tsarist and dedicated to the suppression of even the thought of liberty, equality, and fraternity. But it is not the purpose of an alliance to provide a structure under which governments can grow sentimental over their sympathy for each other or exchange congratulations on the similarities of their views on life, politics, and the universe. Alliances are not friendships. If they were, we would scarcely have any, for national friendships are either illusory or very rare. (National antagonisms are a different matter.) Rather, alliances are in essence concluded so that a country may count on another to fight by its side in times of war, and to support it by a variety of other means in times of peace. A common ideology between allies is a pleasant luxury—it will save the secretary of state from much domestic criticism—but it is not an essential. Mutual advantage is. Common interests, and above all, a common foe, can make allies of nations whose domestic institutions are half a dozen constitutions apart.

These principles certainly applied to the situation between France and Russia. It was true that conflicting systems of government and popular antagonism would delay agreement. But domestic differences would not, in the end, prevent it. With patience, skill, and money, the French government, after 1890, impressed upon the Russians the desirability of cooperating against the common enemy, Germany. The Russians were pleased enough to listen; the French were creating an interesting atmosphere in which to do so. There were French loans to Russia. There was, in 1891, a visit of the French fleet to the naval base of Kronstadt, during which the Tsar, who had made the short trip from St. Petersburg, stood with bared head as the Marseillaise was being played. (Nicholas II would have his day a few years later when the President of France, during another ceremonial visit, had to bare *his* head as the Cossacks marched by.) There were military talks in 1892, cautious but precedent-breaking nonetheless. There was the return visit of the Russian fleet to Toulon in 1893, which set off some enthusiastically pro-Russian demonstrations. There was, finally and most importantly by far, the secret Military Convention signed between Russia and France in 1894. Should any member of the Triple Alliance—Germany, Austria, or Italy—mobilize, the two contracting parties undertook to mobilize as well. Should there be war, they would, under certain conditions, fight side by side. These conditions were clearly defined: Should Germany (or Italy supported by Germany) attack France, Russia would give all military assistance to her new ally; should Germany (or Austria supported by Germany) attack Russia, France would come to the rescue.

The Franco-Russian Military Convention was a landmark in the affairs of Europe. France no longer was in quarantine; the wall that Bismarck built had at long last been breached. More than that, the continental armies that might face each other in a general war would now be fairly even in size. Not that there was any desire for war. The alliance was as genuinely defensive in purpose as any of Bismarck's had been. There was no illusion in Paris

that Russia would now set her armies in motion to liberate Metz and Strasbourg. Nor did any responsible French
statesman, hesitant though he might be to emphasize the
point in public, aim at such a war. What he did want
was what he now had, an end to the days when France,
every step of the way, was automatically outnumbered,
outmaneuvered, and outvoted.

• *Anglo-French Relations and the Shock of Recognition,
1890–1898* If open conflict with Germany was something
the French would rather avoid or at least delay, conflict
with Great Britain was another matter. Animosities and
resentments older than Joan of Arc set the two countries
apart. Modes of life and thought differed profoundly:
Glorious Revolution and The Terror, Burke and Robes-
pierre, as seen from the British side; *Roi Soleil* and Crom-
well, as seen from the French; Declaration of the Rights
of Man and Test Act; and *Coquilles Saint-Jacques* and
fish and chips besides. Nor were differences bridged by
joint diplomatic objectives. Instead, conflicting national
interests as deep as the Channel divided Britain and
France. The century had opened with Great Britain's
implacable stand against Napoleon's France. It threatened to end with an almost equally stubborn opposition
to Republican France, except that this time, the points at
issue concerned colonial rather than continental expansion. England was offended by the idea of further French
gains in North Africa; it had largely been with France
in mind that she had signed the Mediterranean Agreement. England attempted to block France's ambitions in
China, and was willing to fight to prevent any French
presence in or near Egypt. Here, of course, was a problem any European nation expanding overseas faced:
British interests, holdings, and ambitions were now so
vast that wherever on the globe one moved, the British
would feel threatened and prepare to do battle. The
territorial extent of the British Empire and its lifelines

was a credit to British daring, enterprise, and ingenuity. It also was an irritant to others, and a source of much international friction.

Trouble between France and England reached its peak in 1898. For some time, both a French-Ethiopian force, under Captain Marchand, and an Anglo-Egyptian army, under General Kitchener, had been heading for the Sudan. (A junior officer in Kitchener's army, by the way, was Winston Churchill, then twenty-four). The background, briefly, was this: The Sudan had been abandoned by the British after a brief period of occupation in the 1880s, when some surprisingly effective local resistance had persuaded them to depart. Since then, the region had been a sort of political no-man's land, fair game, under the Darwinian laws of European imperialism, to the fittest conqueror. The British now were directing Kitchener's army to retake the Sudan at the same time that the French, setting out from Gabon, were moving toward the region in an effort to reach the Nile. In September 1898, the two forces met at Fashoda, a small town on the Upper Nile.

Wisely, they did not immediately attack. Both forces knew what was at stake. London or Paris would have to give the marching orders. But battle delayed hardly looked like battle denied. Both sides were obdurate. The French would not recall Marchand until the British should make some major colonial concessions elsewhere. The British would listen to no conditions. Kitchener, they said, had retaken the Sudan; let Marchand get out of the way—yield or fight. After six weeks of argument and preparation for war on both sides, the French yielded and Marchand received orders to leave. The British had gambled right. France stood alone, since this was not a conflict in which she could draw on her Russian alliance. France stood ill prepared, racked by the Third Republic's worst *affaire*— the man of the hour was Dreyfus, not Guillaume le Conquérant. And even under different circumstances, it would have made little sense to pour French blood and French resources into the Sudan when Strasbourg was so much closer than Fashoda.

Justify as one might, on sober reflection, the French surrender, it at first spelled national humiliation. Vituperation of the British in the French press was rarely as unrestrained as in 1898. The Nile, for a moment, did seem to matter as much as the Rhine; the British looked more despicable than the Germans. But in the long run, Fashoda brought about an overdue and salutary reappraisal of French foreign policy. Both Britain and France had statesmen of stature during the affair. On the British side, the Marquess of Salisbury, three times prime minister as well as foreign secretary between 1885 and 1902, had shown his acumen by his correct appraisal of the ultimate decision France would reach, although the bluntness of his demands hardly made that decision any easier. On the French side, Delcassé, who only that summer had taken over the foreign ministry, now asked himself a quite basic question: Could France, which was in no position to fight Britain *and* Germany, afford to hate both countries? His answer was that France could not. It was an unsurprising answer, but it was one that his predecessors had never really thought through; if they had, Marchand would not have been sent looking for the Nile. Henceforth, Delcassé would try his best to reach an accommodation with one of the two, and the power he sought to reconcile was Great Britain.

• *Friend or Foe? Anglo-German Relations 1896–1903*
Whether Delcassé would succeed with his new policy was another matter. In France, his decision would be impeded for several years by continuing eruptions of public hostility against the perfidious English. Nor was there much evidence that Britain was eager for any kind of alliance. Had England not fared rather well in splendid isolation, real or imagined? And even if the British should decide

to look for companionship, what about the other major contender for their favors—Germany?

The answer to the first question was easier than the answer to the second. Britain, toward the turn of the century, was becoming more receptive toward alliance offers. A great many troubles were plaguing her, and the globe was proving to be too big a place for even Britain to police alone. The Russians were pursuing alarming ambitions in China. The Turks were in trouble again, and there might soon be another San Stefano. France was getting in Britain's way in Asia and Africa and so were other continental powers. Thus the British could do with some help. They dediced to have another look at their Teutonic cousin; perhaps his manners had improved a bit.

At first, it hardly seemed they had. The mid-1890s were to see one of the worst instances of Anglo-German hostility on record. It began in Africa. The British, for some time, had had their eye on the gold-rich Boer states in the South—the Orange Free State and the Transvaal. At the end of 1895, Dr. Leander Starr Jameson, an administrator in the British South Africa Company, led a raid from British Betsuanaland into the neighboring Transvaal. He hoped to set off a general revolt against the government of Paul Kruger, President of the Transvaal, which should lead to the replacement of Boer with British control. The raid failed badly. There was no revolt, and the Boers quickly and effectively defeated him and his private army.

Continental opinion—not in Holland alone—was very much with Kruger (David usually has a better press than Goliath); British assurances that Jameson had been acting on his own convinced few. But private feelings were one thing, public policy another, and officially, the powers of Europe pursued a policy of neutrality. All, that is, except Germany. In January, 1896, the Kaiser sent a jubilant telegram to Kruger, congratulating him on his success in repelling the invasion "without appeals for the

help of friendly powers." This was a double insult to
London, with its joy over Britain's discomfort, and its
hint that German aid would have been available to
Kruger, and perhaps still was. The telegram was not
wholly a matter of personal impulse, as so many of the
Kaiser's actions were. For one thing, he wished to im-
press the British with the need for compensation in the
event of further colonial expansion. For another, he may
have wished to compel the British into a reappraisal of
their German policy—let them see just how isolated
they were, so that they might draw the proper conclusions
and request admittance to the Triple Alliance.

The British did no such thing, and it is hard to see
how they could have. "My dear William," Queen Victoria
wrote to Berlin, "I feel I cannot refrain from expressing
my deep regret at the telegram you sent President Kruger.
It is considered very unfriendly toward this country, which
I am sure it is not intended to be, and has, I grieve to say,
made a very pointed impression here." Public opinion
ran to sentiments similar to the Queen's, though the language was often less Victorian, and demands could be
heard for closer ties with Russia and France. The government, in a mood as unsubtle as William's, responded by
issuing orders mobilizing a squadron of the British fleet
in the Channel. Browbeating people into friendship had
its dangers.

But alliance hopes were not dead. People fortunately
forget. In the spring of 1898, Joseph Chamberlain, colonial secretary in Salisbury's government, went to see
the German ambassador and proposed the conclusion of
a defensive alliance to him. The German response was
cool. They doubted—correctly so—whether Chamberlain
was in fact speaking for the cabinet; nor were they eager
to offend the Russians, against whom such an alliance
would primarily be directed. Still the idea persisted. The
following year, Chamberlain brought it up again, and this
time, circumstances seemed more auspicious. Britain was

now engaged in a full-scale war against the Boers—the Jameson raid stage was over—and the war was going badly. The Boers were defeating the British, although not forever as it turned out; however, it would take the mighty British Empire nearly three years, from 1899 to 1902, to defeat a handful of emigrant Dutch farmers. And long before it was finished, the Boer War would demonstrate two things: the questionable nature of British military power (jibes about the Russian giant as a colossus on feet of clay, for instance, all at once seemed in dubious taste in England) and the extent and intensity of anti-British sentiment in the world. Many were the people who rejoiced with Kruger over every Boer success: the French saw Fashoda avenged; the Russians would take anyone to their hearts, of course, who beat the British; and the Americans remembered another colonial war, and so it went.

The German government, this time, had learned its lesson. Official Germany policy was one of neutrality. No more telegrams to Kruger; instead, toward the end of 1899, the Kaiser paid a cordial visit to England. It was against the background of this visit, then, that Chamberlain made his second plea for friendship. In a speech he gave in November 1899, at Leicester, he called for nothing less than the establishment of "a new Triple Alliance between the Teutonic race and the two great branches of the Anglo-Saxon race"; nothing else would do as much "to preserve the peace of the world."

The German reaction resembled the response to his previous initiative. The poor progress of the war in South Africa, argued the people who made policy in Berlin, should before long push the British into making a better, or at any rate a more concrete, alliance offer. Brusquely, they turned down the suggestion.

Undaunted, in 1901 Chamberlain tried once more. Again, he failed. The Germans held out for too much: Britain should join the Triple Alliance; for diplomatic

purposes, the Austrians and Italians would have to become Teutons, too. Neither side minded the failure of
negotiations—not then. The British thought that cooperation with Japan might remove some of the immediate pressures in the Far East, and in 1902 concluded an
Anglo-Japanese alliance directed against further Russian
expansion in the area. The British also made the most of
their new cooperation with the United States, which depended on no formal alliance but was, nevertheless, a fact
of diplomatic life ever since the Spanish-American War
had catapulted the United States into world politics. The
Germans still thought that they had all the time in the
world, reasoning that Britain had no choice; surely, she
would never reach an agreement with her arch-rivals
Russia and France. Fashoda and the Crimean War made
comforting memories. No, Britain would come back and
make a more handsome offer.

This brings to mind Fontenelle: "Leibniz never married. He had considered it at the age of fifty, but the
person he had in mind asked for time to reflect. This gave
Leibniz time to reflect, too, and so he never married."

The British proposal, quite possibly, was no more genuine than Leibniz's. What really were they offering the
Germans? They never said. But why did the Germans
not test the British offer by saying yes? The British move
may have been a matter of tactics rather than strategy,
but tactics have a way of developing a momentum of their
own. At any rate, the British, having had time to reflect,
would not woo the Germans again. The balance sheet of
the affair makes for melancholy reading.

Only one thing remained on (or rather near) the positive side: this was an Anglo-German Agreement, concluded in 1898, to divide Portugal's African colonies in
case Portugal should, as was then expected, find itself in
serious financial difficulties and have to pawn parts of
her empire. Actually, it was a perfectly useless treaty.
The following year, the British renewed their ancient

alliance with Portugal. Although the evidence for this is circumstantial rather than direct, they also appear to have provided Lisbon with substantial amounts of pounds sterling; quite suddenly, the country's finances improved, and Angola and Mozambique would remain Portuguese long after most other powers had departed from Africa.

On the negative side, Anglo-German friction would continue nearly unchecked. To begin with, there was the naval race. Starting in 1898, the Germans began building a major navy, arguing that they now had overseas possessions to supply and defend. Continental power no longer sufficed. "Our future," said the Kaiser, "lies on the water." The British, in alarm, reacted by increasing *their* naval building program, whereupon the Germans, after a suitable interval, increased theirs again. And both governments found that the most effective method of persuading their respective parliaments to pass the necessary appropriations was to dramatize the threat from the other side. It was not an atmosphere conducive to friendship.

Then there was the matter of colonial rivalry. Even Bismarck had not been able to hold out forever against the dynamics of imperialism. In the mid-1880s, the Germans began, modestly at first, to acquire African territory. Under William II, all restraints were off: Germany must become a great colonial power! Bismarck's insistence that Germany was a satiated nation was no longer heeded— Germany must show the world that her energies and achievement were second to none. A great power must grow or die; few half-truths have caused as much misery in the world as this.

There was, finally, the matter of economic rivalry with England. The Germans were ambitious to outsell the British in the world's markets, and to redraw some economic spheres of interest as well. In 1899, a German company received a concession to build a railroad from Constantinople to the Persian Gulf, the "Berlin-Baghdad Railway." The project was more grandiose than the available financing, and for monetary as well as diplomatic reasons, the Germans urged the French and British to participate. But by 1903, that effort had failed, since neither the French nor the British would take part. The Russians had fumed about the project from the beginning; they felt that by some ancient right, this was their part of the world. In the case of the French, anti-German sentiment was still something of a reflex action. But that the British, too, should be so dubious about the Germans' motives was a poor omen.

It would be easy to add to these instances of Anglo-German differences. But this is not an encyclopedia of diplomatic crises. Besides, such an unrelieved recitation of troubles can falsify what took place, obscuring the amount of good will that still did exist between the two nations. To give but one instance, the Rhodes scholarships endowed in this same period restricted the recipients to citizens of Great Britain, the United States, and Germany—precisely the combination Joseph Chamberlain had had in mind. And it makes events appear far more inevitable than in fact they were. Many of the points at issue were fairly casual matters at the time. Too many other cares and enmities loomed larger. The British might worry about the Berlin-Baghdad project, but compared with, say a hypothetical Moscow-Baghdad Railway it was a minor care. It is only in retrospect that the various instances of Anglo-German friction look so momentous. Hard as it is to avoid in the writing of history, *post hoc ergo propter hoc* remains one of the most basic of fallacies. Still, one consequence of it all was that unlike Leibniz, the British now were willing to try marriage—but with a different partner.

• *Entente Cordiale, 1904* In 1900, Lord Lansdowne had succeeded Salisbury as British foreign secretary. Salisbury had held out, with Washingtonian conviction, against any entangling alliances. Lansdowne did not. It was not that he was any fonder of alliances as such. It was rather that he had taken a new and sharp look at certain facts. What he saw, in the first place, was the far from splendid sort of isolation in which England found herself. What he also saw was that the major problems of the period were not continental but colonial. It was overseas, in Africa and Asia, that the principal pressures and conflicts were accumulating. Had it been otherwise, England would have had no cause to abandon nonalignment, since in Europe, she held precisely what she wanted: the perfect balance of power between the two rival alliances, the Franco-Russian, and the Austro-German-Italian. But overseas, in the pursuit of imperialism, she faced too many enemies; she also faced the danger that these enemies—Russia, France, and Germany—might one day unite against her. Britain, Lansdowne felt, would have to come to a settlement with at least one ally.

But which one? Russia seemed irreconcilable, her appetite limitless: Manchuria, Korea, Persia, the Dardanelles, and who could tell what else the Tsar might want. Germany made a better, and certainly a more likeable prospect, but the Germans had just demonstrated their reluctance to come to an agreement. This left France. Here, then, was the opportunity Delcassé had been waiting for, and he made splendid use of it, showing now exactly the sort of moderation, patience, tact, and comprehension of essentials that the Germans had so lacked during the three Chamberlain episodes. And mood and circumstance were right. It was the period of Edward VII, who, since succeeding Queen Victoria in 1901, had done a magnificent job of dispelling a major portion of anti-British feeling in France by his obvious enjoyment of things pleasantly French. (Also, Lansdowne, on his mother's side, could claim descent from Talleyrand, but that fact may deserve no more than parenthetical mention. Sir Eyre Crowe, one of the senior permanent officials in the foreign office and its most persistently, almost hysterically, anti-German member, was half German.) In the spring of 1904, negotiations begun the year before, were complete. Formally, the agreement reached consisted of a number of separate and concrete accords; informally, it would become known in its entirety as the *Entente Cordiale*. And "Cordial Understanding" was a good term, for the two countries were agreeing to settle all outstanding colonial issues between them, minor ones and major ones alike, from disputes over customs duties in Madagascar to fishing rights off the coast of Newfoundland. (The latter, by the way, proved to be more resistant to resolution than any other single problem discussed.) But the core of the argument dealt with Egypt and Morocco. France agreed to give England a free hand in Egypt; the British, in return, agreed that Morocco should be in the French sphere. There were to be no more tests of strength and temper over ill-defined regions of interest —no more Fashodas.

Was the alliance directed against Germany? Was it, in fact, an alliance? The negotiators involved could say no to both questions, though not with an altogether easy conscience. It was true that Germany was not mentioned and that the *Entente* ostensibly dealt with colonial, not with European affairs. It was also true that there were no provisions for assistance in case of war, the usual characteristic of a major alliance. Yet the risk was there that the Moroccan provision might involve England on the side of France, since the argument over Morocco could— and would—as easily be one between France and Germany as between France and England. Above all, Britain *had* emerged from isolation, and no matter how cautious and limited the documents that attributed to that fact might be, she had come out on the side of France, not of Germany. Time now would tell whether the *Entente*—as Delcassé but perhaps not Lansdowne wished—would indeed assume the character of an alliance.

• *Testing the Entente: Russo-Japanese War, Moroccan Crisis, Björkö, and the Matter of Staff Talks, 1904–1906*
For the moment, it appeared as though the *Entente* might

not survive at all, let alone develop into a firm alliance. Within six months of its conclusion, England went to the edge of war with France's eastern ally, Russia. The setting was provided by the Russo-Japanese War of 1904–1905.

The rivalry between Russia and Japan was old and bitter; both were seeking to profit from the decline of China by expanding into Manchuria and Korea. Early in 1904, the Japanese chose major war over minor skirmishes. Without warning and without a declaration of war, they attacked the Russian fleet at Port Arthur. The Russians, outfought and outthought, decided to bring up their reserves; they would send their Baltic fleet half way around the world to defeat the Japanese. On its fantastic journey to the Far East, that fleet won one victory. Shortly after starting out from port in October 1904, it encountered what looked to its officers like a group of Japanese torpedo boats near the Dogger Bank in the North Sea. The Russians opened fire, missing many, but managing to sink one. The pity of it was that Russian marksmanship was even this good, for the Japanese men-of-war in truth were British fishing boats.

The British were incensed. Suddenly the two countries were as close to war as they had been at the time of San Stefano. It was a prospect that, elating though it might be to many a Britisher and Russian, horrified Delcassé. Using all his powers of persuasion, he kept France's two allies from each other's throats. Grudgingly, the Russians admitted their error, promised compensation, and even put the responsible officers ashore. The rest of the fleet, minus the myopic officers, sailed on, to be annihilated by the Japanese at the battle of Tsushima.

Soon after that battle, in the fall of 1905, peace was negotiated on neutral territory in Portsmouth, New Hampshire. (A considerable part in arranging the negotiations had been played by President Theodore Roosevelt; his successful mediation would bring him the Nobel Peace Prize in 1906.) Considering Russia's performance in the war, the peace terms were lenient; even so, Portsmouth put a temporary stop to Russia's ambitions in the Far East.

The consequences of the Russo-Japanese War for European diplomacy were twofold. In the first place, the Dogger Bank incident marked a crucial point in Anglo-Russian relations. Had the British retaliated, as easily they might, there would be many a learned volume now explaining how the great Anglo-Russian War of 1904 was a logical and inevitable development of decades of friction between London and St. Petersburg. And indeed, if some sort of apparatus for the precise measurement of hostility between nations were to exist, Anglo-Russian relations, in the half century or so before 1904, might receive its highest score. But, narrowly or not, war had been avoided, and the two countries found that they could talk as well as shout, particularly when they could draw on the offices of as good an intermediary as France. The second consequence, connected, of course, with the first, was that Russia was temporarily in a chastened mood. The direct domestic result of the bungled war was the Revolution of 1905. Tsardom would have a difficult enough time merely to survive. Thoughts of expansion, at least in the Far East, would have to wait. The attention of Russia's policy makers, once the immediate crisis was over, turned to Europe again, an attitude that did not at all displease the French.

But actually how strong was France's understanding with England? The Germans decided to find out, now that the happy prospect of a battle between France's eastern and northern allies had vanished. In March 1905, the Kaiser, on a Mediterranean cruise, landed at Tangiers in Spanish Morocco, and publicly declared Germany's support for Moroccan independence and integrity. Diplomacy's public language is often circuitous, and William did not, with these words, mean to express any true support for Morocco's native regime, which was hopelessly ineffectual. What he did mean to suggest was that Germany had as much of a claim to Morocco as any other greedy European power. To make that point even clearer, the Germans followed up the Imperial speech with a demand for an international conference on Morocco. The French, they calculated, were sure to be outvoted in such a conference, in which Germany would demand an Open Door policy for Morocco. Spain and Italy, they reasoned, were sufficiently jealous of France to vote with Germany; Russia was exhausted and dependent on Germany's good will; Austria-Hungary was Germany's firm ally; and the British were anxious to safeguard their profitable trade with Morocco and thus to favor a policy of the Open Door. Even if Germany's direct gains from such a conference should be slight since there were too many contenders for Moroccan privileges, the diplomatic isolation of France would once again appear as plainly as in Bismarck's days.

The French, considerably worried, went out of their way to suggest some compromise. In May, the French government offered the Germans a port on the coast of Morocco; in June, the cabinet dropped Delcassé, who alone was holding out for a hard line against Germany. The Germans were adamant; they wanted their conference. Their wish no longer could be resisted, and early in 1906, in the Spanish town of Algeciras, the conference convened. But the Germans had pushed their luck too far, and hardly anything worked out the way they had expected. The British were very much disturbed by what they rightly took to be a case of German bullying. The Russians were much more intrigued by what the British rather than the German delegates had to say. The Americans showed a decided preference for accents that reminded them of Lafayette rather than of the Hessians. The Spaniards and Italians rediscovered their Latin bonds as they listened to French references to compensation, a topic the Germans had not had the wit to pay much attention to. When the votes were counted, Germany was in a minority in every instance; none but Austria-Hungary would side with her. Except for its relatively small Spanish section, Morocco, in effect, was to be open to French economic and political penetration. Even more important than the technicalities of the settlement was the cooperation between the French and British delegations at Algeciras. The Germans had meant the conference to be a test of the *Entente*. It was, except that the results were all wrong. Germany, not France stood in isolation. The *Entente* had emerged stronger than before.

Overplaying a hand remained a German specialty. In the early stages of the Moroccan crisis, in July 1905, Tsar and Kaiser, pleasure-cruising in the Baltic, met near the Finnish island of Björkö. William, at the time, was still savoring Delcassé's fall; Nicholas was still brooding over the humiliation of the Dogger Bank episode. The Kaiser, visiting the Tsar's yacht, brought along the draft of a treaty, which, he told Nicholas, "I happen to have quite by chance in my pocket." The treaty provided for a defensive alliance between Germany and Russia against attack from any other power in Europe. In other words, it was a treaty that would have neutralized Russia as France's ally. How would his cousin Nicholas like to sign it, right then and there? "It would be a very nice souvenir of our *entrevue.*" Nicholas did want to sign it. "Bright tears of joy" wrote William, "stood in my eyes." Just like that, Germany and Russia were allies again.

But not quite just like that. When the two sovereigns returned to dry land, they were astonished by the political reception to their action. The German Chancellor, Prince Bernhard von Bülow, at first would have no part of the agreement. He had no objection to a treaty with Russia, but this was not the form he had in mind. Bülow was no model of either statesmanship or courage, but this particular instance of Imperial casualness was too much even for him. Only a desperate plea from William—"think of my poor wife and children"—kept him from resigning the chancellorship. Thus, Bülow decided he would make the best of a bad opening move and let the treaty stand. It was a pointless decision, because in Russia, the Tsar had meanwhile had to listen to his foreign ministry's obvious argument that the Björkö agreement plainly violated the spirit of the French alliance. With some embarrassment, he wrote the Kaiser that the treaty could not go into effect quite yet. Also, might it not be possible to add a few words stating that the agreement was to be suspended in the event of war between France and Germany?

Of course, no such addition was possible. "What is signed is signed and God is witness of it!" replied William. His protest went unheard, and the treaty never did go into effect. All that remained were injured feelings. "Two great princes who wish to live in amity," Philippe de Commynes had written half a millenium earlier, "should never meet, but send each other good and wise envoys."

The French now showed they had retained a good deal of Commynes' good sense. At the end of 1905, while the Moroccan situation was still critical and peace by no means certain, they asked the British for a promise of military support in case of war with Germany. Sir Edward Grey, who at just that moment had succeeded Lansdowne as foreign secretary (a post he would hold until 1916, longer than any other foreign secretary ever continuously held office) did not feel that this was a promise he had either the inclination or the authority to make. What he did do, however, was to authorize informal military conversations between the British and the French, conversations that began in 1906 and continued until Sarajevo replaced them with other arrangements.

No binding agreements were ever signed in the course

of these talks, no pledges of aid exchanged. In fact, the British cabinet would not even learn of their existence until 1912, the British public not until 1914. However, the military experts involved did agree on a number of very specific details of military cooperation, *if* such cooperation should ever be called for, from the size and deployment of a British expeditionary force to an understanding concerning the most efficient use of both fleets— the British were to guard the North Sea, the French, the Mediterranean. Theoretically, then, both nations preserved perfect freedom of action. Actually, England's moral obligation to France increased as the talks went on. The British would not very well ask the French to deploy their navy in the Mediterranean without assuming *some* implied responsibility for intercepting a German fleet heading for Dunkerque or Cherbourg. Nor was it really feasible to carry on, over a period of eight years, talks involving some of the most precise details of possible military cooperation without giving the French—the phrase is Grey's—"an expectation of support."

In part through German clumsiness, in part through French ingenuity, sometimes by gradual stages, sometimes by sharp crises, the *Entente* had turned into something startlingly like an alliance.

• *Triple Entente: The Anglo-Russian Understanding of 1907* The trend from *Entente* to alliance suggested to the British the wisdom of reassessing their relations with Russia. Avoiding friction with one's ally's ally is a fairly basic tenet of statecraft. Besides, there was always the fear that the next time Tsar and Kaiser met, they might come up with another, better thought out, Björkö agreement. But that was not the side Britain wanted Russia to be on. Considering Germany's apparent designs on the Near East, the British could use an ally who was in a position to oppose the prospective builders of a railroad from Berlin to Baghdad. Moreover, now that Russia had been expelled from China, and thus some

definite points of Anglo-Russian friction reduced, the
possibilities of agreement between London and St. Petersburg looked better than they had for a long time.

Encouraged by the French, the British, after Algeciras,
urged the Russians to consider the advantages of a *rapprochement*. The Russians acted reluctant. The Tsar was
preoccupied with the problem of the regime's domestic
survival, and the revolution of 1905 was still a bad and
vivid memory. He also was concerned lest he give offense
to the Germans. Britain might have the world's greatest
navy and shiniest gold reserve, but Britain was far away.
Germany was a neighbor. But then the British held out
a lure too sweet to resist. They might, just might, change
their views on the Dardanelles and favor the opening of
the Straits to Russian shipping in war as well as in peace.
(The Russo-Japanese War had just demonstrated again
how galling the provision was which closed the Straits in
the event of war. Russia's Black Sea fleet had been im-
prisoned by the Straits, and hence wholly useless.) In
truth, the British promise was vague, but the Russians
chose not to read it that way. In 1907, they signed a
formal agreement with Great Britain. The agreement was
similar to the Anglo-French *Entente* of 1904 in that, on
the face of it, the two powers were merely settling certain
outstanding specific colonial issues between them rather
than entering into a military alliance. It was similar, too,
in that the whole of the agreement was really greater
than the sum of its parts.

Specifically, what the Anglo-Russian accord of 1907
settled was the fate of Persia, Tibet, and Afghanistan.
Both sides agreed to stay out of Tibet, while Britain was
to have a free hand in Afghanistan. Persia was divided
into spheres of influence: the North went to Russia, the
South to Britain, and a neutral zone in the middle provided a buffer between the two. It was imperialism at its
bluntest as well as at its most hypocritical: "a mutual self-
denying ordinance recognizing Persian independence,"
Grey piously called it.

No matter; what counted was that Britain and Russia had agreed to settle their principal points of imperialistic conflict by negotiation, as Britain and France had done three years earlier. And amicable and pacific as the agreement was, there was implicit in it a considerable element of political danger. Hitherto, Russia's ambitions in the Balkans and in the Near East had been restrained by the powers, notably by England. Now, Russia had reason to assume that she might some day count on Western aid and comfort in the pursuit of her aims. Beyond that, what some writers have called a diplomatic revolution had taken place. The Triple Alliance of Germany, Austria-Hungary, and Italy (or rather the Dual Alliance, for Italy's reliability had become a matter of justified doubt) after 1907 found itself faced by the Triple *Entente* of France, Great Britain, and Russia. It was the triumph of France. Utterly alone in 1871, a generation later she was *à trois* in a world ruled by five powers. To quote Bismarck again, it was the kind of union which "would provide the basis for a coalition against us more dangerous than any other which Germany could possibly face."

• *Bosnia and the Annexation Crisis of 1908–1909* The country that initially courted conflict with the new coalition was not Germany, however, but Austria-Hungary. In 1908, the Austrians thought that they might follow the first step they had taken in 1878 with a second. (When the Austrians talked about deliberate speed, the stress was on the adjective.) They would annex the provinces of Bosnia and Herzegovina which they had been given to "occupy and administer" at the Congress of Berlin. There were several good reasons for their annexation—for instance, the need to clarify the legal status of Bosnia-Herzegovina, and the desire to demonstrate to the Turks that returning the provinces was out of the question. But probably the strongest single reason was that held by Count Lexa von Aehrenthal who, two years earlier, had acceded to the foreign ministry, and who felt very strongly that Austria, to survive, needed to show that she was still capable of action.

Aehrenthal, while ready to pursue a policy that contained its share of risks, was not a reckless man; he would first probe the Russian reaction. In September 1908, he met his Russian counterpart, Alexander Izvolski, at Buchlau in Moravia. Izvolski was by no means delighted at Aehrenthal's plans, but he was willing to strike a bargain: Russia would not oppose annexation if Austria, in return, would support the opening of the Straits to Russian warships. Aehrenthal agreed, although by design or not, he volunteered very little information about the precise date of Austria's intended action on either Bosnia or the Straits.

A month later, in October 1908, the Austrians proclaimed to the world that they were annexing Bosnia and Herzegovina. Izvolski was furious. He felt that Aehrenthal had broken his word: it had been his understanding at Buchlau that annexation was in the fairly distant future and would follow rather than antecede a new Straits settlement. Angrier even than the Russian foreign minister were the Serbians. They had had their own designs in this area; the region's citizens were fellow Slavs. Crowds in Belgrade called for war. Their government seemed willing to oblige them.

Britain and France rallied to support their Russian ally. Austria's action was a violation of the Treaty of Berlin and should be opposed—but not to the point of war. This, on sober thought, was the way the Russians reacted too, since they knew they were in no position to fight a European war this soon after the debacle of 1905. They also knew that Austria could count on German aid —reluctant aid, to be sure, for Berlin had had as little advance warning of Aehrenthal's action as anyone else, but aid nonetheless. Thus, galling though the task might be, St. Petersburg intervened to restrain Belgrade.

Ultimately, when the crisis was over in 1909, war had

been averted, but hardly anyone had gained. A Russian attempt to use the crisis to obtain concessions on the Straits foundered on British opposition. The ties of the Triple *Entente* were not that firm; neither its letter nor its spirit provided for British support of all of Russia's national aspirations. St. Petersburg's firmer ally, Serbia, would not forget or forgive 1908, disliking the Russians for their lack of support, but hating the Austrians even more. Austria, it was true, managed to keep Bosnia-Herzegovina, but the price, a cash compensation to Turkey aside, was Russian enmity. Those Austrians, and there were many, who had argued against changing the status of 1878, legally awkward though it might be, had been right. Less ambition on Aehrenthal's part—Talleyrand's *pas de zèle*—would have served Austria better.

• *The Panther's Leap: The Second Moroccan Crisis of 1911* A period of relative calm and of a search for accommodation followed the annexation affair. Not all was a blind rush toward catastrophe, of crisis pursuing crisis in pre-1914 Europe, nor was what had taken place in 1908 and 1909 that corrosive to international good will. Tranquillity is harder to record than trouble, of course, and general and genuine accommodation would remain elusive. There would still take place, in the five years between Aehrenthal's coup and Princip's shots, one major crisis and several minor wars. Any serious diplomatic narrative must mention them, but it should also note, even if in this cursory fashion only, the existence of normalcy, peace, and a sense of proportion on the part of many of Europe's statesmen.

The major crisis involved Morocco. The Algeciras conference had given France considerable rights in Morocco, although these rights were hedged with provisions that recognized the continuing economic interests of others in the region. In 1911, when a native revolt led to open French military intervention, the Germans took the op-

portunity to remind Paris that Morocco was still nominally independent, and that they could set some limits to
French expansion. Early in July, 1911, the German gunboat *Panther* appeared at the Moroccan port of Agadir,
ostensibly to protect German citizens there, but actually
to promote much larger German ambitions, although
these did not involve Morocco itself. The Germans had
no designs there. What they did want was compensation
elsewhere. They would, they confided to the French, be
willing to recognize a French protectorate over Morocco
if in return they were to receive the entire French Congo.

The demand was immoderate, the method childish.
Gunboat diplomacy is a game for experts, and the Germans were amateurs. The *"Panther's* leap," as the press
came to see it, gave German diplomacy an image of crude-
ness and brutality. It also caused a great deal of alarm
in Britain, as the British dreaded the thought of seeing
the Germans this close to Gibraltar. The Kaiser, they
thought (wrongly, as it turned out) meant to turn Agadir
into a German naval base. Thus on July 21, 1911, David
Lloyd George, in the course of a speech he gave at London's Mansion House, repaid the Germans in coin as
undiplomatic as that they had used themselves.

Lloyd George, Chancellor of the Exchequer since 1908,
was in a bad mood as far as Germany was concerned. He
had long been an advocate of a whole series of social reforms, from health insurance to old age pensions, reforms
that, no matter how socially desirable, cost a great deal of
money. Yet a disproportionate amount of the British
budget had to be allocated to naval armaments. The
Germans were engaged in a major program for building
dreadnoughts—the newest of the "all-big-guns" battleships—in which Britain could not afford to be overtaken.
Anger at both the implications of the naval race and at
German heavy-handedness over Agadir found an outlet
then in Lloyd George's Mansion House speech, when he
said:

I believe it is essential in the highest interests, not only of this country, but of the world, that Great Britain should at all hazards maintain her place and prestige among the Great Powers of the world. . . . If a situation were to be forced upon us in which peace could only be preserved by the surrender of the great and beneficent position Britain has won by centuries of heroism and advancement, by allowing Britain to be treated where her interests were vitally affected as though she were of no account in the Cabinet of nations, then I say emphatically that peace at that price would be a humiliation intolerable for a great country like ours to endure.

This was not the public language of diplomacy, especially in a case where no direct British interest was at stake, and the Germans had some right to be offended. But British support for France was clear, even if in subsequent talks the tone was more genteel. This part of the *Entente* was holding. The Germans chose to come to terms. In November 1911, after a great deal of difficult bargaining, agreement was reached: the French ceded some worthless strips of territory in the Congo to the Germans; in return, the Germans gave France a free hand in Morocco and withdrew their naval units.

Again, as in the Bosnian crisis, it was a solution short of war, but one short of giving general satisfaction as well. Many Frenchmen were displeased because a part of their colonial empire had been surrendered to the Germans. Many Britishers were supplied with new grounds for disliking their transaquatic cousins. Many Germans thought the Congolese gains hardly worth the risks and trouble taken, and right they were, for another parallel needs to be drawn between the Bosnian and Second Moroccan Crises: both involved prestige politics at its very worst. Neither Austria's position in Bosnia, nor Germany's in North Africa, by any reasonable calculation were worth a war, and no power, in fact, seriously contemplated war. (Serbia, in 1908, was the exception to the rule.) Yet war was talked about much too freely. Thus, through a combination of maladroit diplomacy, ill-advised publicity, and entangling alliances, minor matters were turned into major issues of national pride and international concern. Still, Europe had survived both affairs, and the next test of nerves would come from a quite different source and, incidentally, would prove that part at least of the new alliance system was still quite capable of being disentangled.

• *The Troubles of Turkey* THE TRIPOLITANIAN WAR, 1911–1912 The different source first was Italy, and after that four Balkan nations. Rome's appetite was growing with the French eating. The Italians, after watching the success of France in Morocco, decided in 1911 to act on an old plan of theirs. They would annex Tripoli. Tripoli, aside from the fact that the Turks who held it were weak, had little to recommend it. Its resources were negligible, its inhabitants quarrelsome, its soil largely desert. It was, in sum, such an undesirable area that neither had the French cared to expand into it from Tunisia, nor the British from Egypt. If it had not been a matter of keeping up with the Schmidts, the Dubois, and the Joneses, it is hard to see what could have attracted the Italians to Tripoli.

But the game of keeping up was precisely the one the Italians wished to play, and they had prepared the diplomatic ground very carefully. They had long ago informed most major powers of their intentions and purchased their approval by various means. In the case of France, the Italians had, as early as 1902, agreed to remain neutral in any war in which France was the aggrieved party, to which they had added an accord that as Tripoli was to be within Italy's sphere of influence, so Morocco was to be within that of France. In the case of Russia, the equally secret Racconigi Agreement of 1909 (signed at that small Piedmontese town near Turin) provided for a comparable trade: Italy would back the Russian position on the matter of the Straits; Russia would support Italy's designs on Tripoli. *Quid pro quo,* although the delicate question remained of how these agreements might be reconciled with Italy's professed adherence to the Triple Alliance. Here was Italy, bound under the terms of the regularly renewed Triple Alliance of 1882 to come to the aid of Germany and Austria, concluding secret agreements with the potential enemies of her allies and, in the case of France, very clearly promising neutrality.

There was, the Italians knew, no way of reconciling the two sets of obligations. Italy was changing sides, and moving into the French camp.

A good argument could be made for the shift. The Habsburgs were hardly Italy's natural ally, and the French, who were present in North Africa, were in a position to offer more than the Germans, who were not. Alliances are not eternal; public assurances of national friendship need be no more sincere than the word "sincerely" used in closing a letter. Even so, there remains something shabby about Italy's maneuvers. In mood and essence, they were too naïvely Machiavellian. Everything in *The Prince* clearly depends on the manner in which it is executed, and the Italian approach lacked style and elegance. Whoever offered Italy more sand could have her in partnership. The sad fact was that prewar Italy missed Cavour's intelligence as badly as Germany missed Bismarck's.

For the moment, however, there was still room for illusions. The Italians did well in the Tripolitanian war; they were gaining what they had set out to acquire. (It should be noted, however, that not all Italians were enthusiastic about the war with Turkey. Among those most violent in opposing it was a Socialist newspaper editor who, in the course of his public campaign against it, called the national flag "a rag, to be planted on a dunghill" and who soon thereafter found himself in prison for this particular contribution to the war effort; his name was Benito Mussolini.) By 1912, the Turks acknowledged that they had lost the war and formally surrendered Tripoli to the Italians, who renamed it Libya, a change that would neither make the natives more friendly nor the soil more fertile. Of all the imperialist ventures undertaken by a European power, Tripoli-Libya would turn out to be the most plainly unprofitable.

• THE BALKAN WARS 1912–1913   The Tripoli-Libya venture would also be one of the most contagious, for the ease with which the Italians had won their victories led a number of Balkan states to decide on taking action of their own against Turkey. In 1912, Bulgaria, Serbia, Montenegro, and Greece forgot their mutual quarrels long enough to unite for war against Ottoman rule in the Balkans. The Russians, to whom their enemy's enemy was a friend, were happy to encourage them. Relatively little urging was required and the stakes were high. Macedonia and Albania, all that remained of the Turkish imperial presence in Europe, might fall to the attacker. The moment seemed propitious. The Italians had opened the gates, and it would be wise to follow them in without too much delay. They might swing shut again, since not long before a disquieting event had taken place in Constantinople. A group of Young Turk reformers, eager to bring their nation into the modern age, had seized many positions of power in 1908, and it seemed essential to move before their reforms had a chance to go into effect. (It was a thought that had played its part in the Austrian annexation of Bosnia as well.) Turkey, as its poor showing against Italy demonstrated, was still satisfactorily weak, and the Tripolitanian war, while coming to a close, was still engaging Constantinople's attention on another continent. This, then, was the time to strike.

Militarily, the four Balkan allies did exceedingly well in their war against Turkey, defeating their enemy wherever they engaged him. Diplomatically, they did less well.

The powers were agreeable to letting them divide Macedonia, but Austria successfully objected to allowing Serbia
and Montenegro to acquire Albania. To give Belgrade
this much new territory and access to the sea as well,
thought the Austrians, would make for too frightening an
increase in Serbian power. Still, it was victory. When the
peace treaty was signed in May 1913, Turkey had ceased
to be a European power.

Within a few weeks of the peace, normalcy returned, as
the Balkan nations fell to bickering with one another
again. None thought the division of the spoils a just one.
At the end of June 1913, the Bulgarians resorted to direct
action and attacked the Greeks and Serbians. It was an
unwise move. Within a very short time, they were outnumbered five to one. Montenegro, allied to Serbia, joined
the anti-Bulgarian side. So did Rumania, hitherto neutral, but now scenting the chance to recover the Southern
Dobrudja, which had been accorded to Bulgaria at the
Congress of Berlin. So, for similarly non-philanthropic
reasons did Turkey, yesterday's enemy of Serbia and
Greece. In August 1913, the Second Balkan War was
over, and the Bulgarians were not the winners. Under
the terms of the Treaty of Bucharest, which formally
ended it, much of the Macedonian territory claimed by
Bulgaria went to Greece and Serbia, while the Dobrudja
went to Rumania. Albania escaped undivided. Instead,
it was established as a nominally independent state, which
would become celebrated, for years to come, for the quality of its political instability.

Why retell this story of the two Balkan Wars, confus-
ing even in this barest outline? Not because they were
of vast direct significance in the affairs of the major
powers. Balkan quarrels were not that crucial. It is told
again, rather, because it contains some of the germs of
1914: the expansionist ambitions of the new nations of
Southeastern Europe; the unashamed use of blunt force
to settle territorial conflicts; the encouragement, on Rus-

sia's part, of Balkan violence; the opposition, on Austria's part, to Serbia's unchecked growth; the dissatisfaction of Bulgaria with the Macedonian settlement. None of these, to reiterate the point, were matters of cosmic import. Yet all of them would be a part of the background to the crime of Gavrilo Princip.

• *Road to Disaster? 1871–1914 in Perspective* The Balkan quarrels were a *part* of the background, and, in this case, the qualifying phrase is more than just another instance of the historian's tendency toward automatic equivocation. For no solution of Balkan problems can be imagined that would have pleased everyone concerned and that would not have contained some seeds of future conflict. Each of the rival aspirations—Bulgaria's, Serbia's, Montenegro's, Rumania's, Greece's, even Turkey's—had its historic or ethnic justification. Claims and rights were so contradictory and so entangled that the wisest and most disinterested of judges imaginable could never establish one side's justice except at the cost of another's injustice. No matter what the solution, resentment would flourish. Tragedy, in the Hegelian definition, is not the conflict of right with wrong, but of right with right. This, indeed, was one of the basic aspects of Southeastern Europe's tragedy. Hence, while the aftermath of the Balkan Wars—with Serbia anxious for further aggrandizement, Bulgaria impatient to overturn the verdict of Bucharest, Austria profoundly concerned over the future designs of both Russia and Serbia—had some quite direct connection with Sarajevo, no other conceivable outcome would have brought a guarantee of stability either.

Then, too, the Balkans were Europe's periphery, not its center. The happy citizen in Goethe's *Faust* had put it well:

> I know nought better on a Sunday or a holiday
> Than chat of war and warlike pother

> When off in Turkey, far away
> These people clash and fight with one another.
> We stand beside the window, drain our glasses
> And see how each gay vessel down the river passes
> Then in the evening homeward wend our ways
> Blessing with joy sweet peace and peaceful ways.

That was the way it still was. The world was not that interdependent. Balkan plots were subplots, and it would take an exceptional set of circumstances to change this.

What, though, of the conflicts between the major powers, whose story has just filled so many of these pages? What of colonial rivalries, of near-war over Morocco, of Strasbourg unforgotten, of dreadnoughts, of the adventures of Italy? Two things need to be said about these, if we are to put them into some kind of perspective. The first is that there was some consolation in their very seriousness. Europe's diplomats were quite as capable as later historians of seeing the dangers they faced, and since none of them desired general war, the incentive for finding some formula for peaceful compromise was considerable. (That such a formula was often agreed on only at the last possible moment was another matter, but then, the only new thing about brinkmanship is the term itself.) To quote Jules Cambon, in a report he sent from Berlin in January 1912:

The failing health of the Emperor of Austria, the far-reaching plans attributed to the Heir-Apparent, the Tripoli War, the desire of the Italian government to extricate itself from the difficulties it had brought upon itself by mixing the disputes of others with its own, Bulgaria's ambitions, the threat of trouble in Macedonia, the difficulties in Persia, the shock to the credit of China, all pointed to serious disorders in the near future and the only hope was that the gravity of the danger might lead to its being averted.

The second point worth making is that while there were many things that went wrong in Europe between

1871 and 1914 (Cambon's list is only a sampling, after all), there were perhaps equally many that went right. Germany did restrain her ambitions for two decades. Britain and France showed that no matter how ancient their enmities and how present their imperial rivalries, it was perfectly possible to find a formula for accommodation. Germany and France reached no similar agreement, yet talks between the two never ceased. Strong forces in both countries worked toward reducing tensions, and by 1914, they had reached an understanding concerning spheres of economic interest, while the President of the Republic broke a habit of hostility of over four decades and came to dine at the German Embassy in Paris. Great Britain and Germany, real though their naval and colonial rivalries were, similarly continued to explore the possibilities of a *détente,* whose concrete results, in 1914, were an agreement to construct new battleships at a rate of 16 to 10 in England's favor, and an understanding under which the two nations agreed again to divide Portugal's African possessions to the exclusion of Europe's other powers. Russia did act to curb Belgrade in 1908. The Austrian government, for its part, did dismiss the chief of the general staff in Vienna when he advocated preventive war against Serbia.

In fact, the concept of war itself as a rational and legitimate means of policy was being questioned. The Hague Convention of 1899 not only initiated some serious international discussions on the limitation of armaments, it also established a Permanent Court of Arbitration, which first convened in 1901, and by its existence offered a juridical alternative to force. The list of what went right could be extended. But it may be enough to say that it was primarily in obeisance to the conventions of historiography, which tend to deal with crisis rather than normalcy, and to stress disaster over triumph, that these pages have had so much more to say about Morocco than the Hague.

However, these conventions, like most, are not without reason. Had all been harmony and a search for peaceful answers, the story's end would not have been so bloody. Knowing the end, we have good cause to look for the road that led to the precipice. Yet we may not find it, or we may find too many roads. For knowing what happened in 1914, we tend to fit together events and trends that have no necessary connection—Fashoda, Morocco, the Balkan Wars. We present them in sequence, saying in effect: this is the mosaic (or the road, if we would rather not switch metaphors). Yet all we have may be no more than individual pieces that assume a semblance of coherence only in retrospect, and through the techniques of historial narration which require an impression of order even where none may in truth exist. In actual fact, there was very little connection between Bulgaria, 1913, and Belgium, 1914. Nonetheless, we begin with 1871, and either imply or state outright that this was where the road started that led from Franco-Prussian War to World War, from the loss of Alsace-Lorraine in one bitter conflict to its recovery in another.

But why even this starting point, quite aside from the question of how the events in the four and a half decades following it are truly and inherently related to one another? Why not begin in 1815, or in 1789, or in 1689 with the French destruction of Heidelberg, or in 1648 with the peace of Westphalia? The answer is not that 1871 was such a decisive date. It is rather that—the human need to find order and meaning and some cause and effect relationship apart—1871 is a convenience and an academic convention. We must begin somewhere, and by academic consensus, we customarily begin with the peace of Frankfurt. But let us at least note that history may be an argument without beginning as well as without end. "The origins," reads a sentence in the preface to a recent book on the battle of Stalingrad, "go back 30 days or 300 years."

The world, as it approached 1914, was not in a com-

pletely deplorable state. Crises were not much graver than
they were in years past or in years to come. True, the two
decades prior to Bismarck's fall were, all in all, happier and saner, than the two and a half that followed them.
True, the conflict for power was terribly naked at times,
and the fact that its worst consequences had usually, and
at one minute to twelve, been worded off, had bred an
atmosphere of overconfidence in which some people were
willing to take some fearful risks. Yet crises are diplomacy's daily bread, and diplomats have had to cope with
more vexing ones without abdicating their responsibilities
to the generals. One may easily argue, for instance, that
international affairs were fraught with far more dangers
in the half century or so that followed the Napoleonic
wars. It was in this period that Europe had to adjust to
revolutionary changes in its frontiers and its balance of
power; that the continent was divided into ideological
camps, Liberal versus Reactionary; that the decline of
Turkey assumed its most dramatic form, with Greece,
Serbia, Rumania, and Bulgaria achieving autonomy or
independence by bloody rebellion; and that Italy achieved
unification through blood and iron. Yet, throughout it
all, there had been an absence of general war.

To understand, then, the causes of the First World War,
we will need to survey two other topics. One concerns
the basic, underlying issues that made for conflict between the powers. The other concerns the immediate
crisis that led to a state of war in 1914.

3 Europe on the Eve: How Deep the Trouble?

According to one report (there was no Hansard then, and we rely on rumor) a member of the Polish *Sejm* once rose to stop the flow of an afternoon's particularly euphoric rhetoric. "Gentlemen," he said, "if everything is so good why is everything so bad?" If so much was right with pre-1914 Europe, how could a second-rate Balkan plot set off a first-rate catastrophe? Were there not, in truth, organic weaknesses that plagued Europe and lowered the continent's powers of resistance to a perilous degree?

What were the troubles, deeper than the immediate crisis, that affected Europe before 1914? We might do well to have at least a look at the principal diagnoses made by various writers: at the state system, at the system of alliances, at major sources of conflict both overseas and closer to the center, at the role of public opinion and the press, and finally, at the acceptance of war as a means of policy.

• *A Matter of Political Organization: The National State*
Some writers have suggested that one truly basic factor that made war an ever-present prospect in 1914, (as in 1814, as well as on the day that this is being read) was nothing less than the national state—a form of political organization accepted by a vast majority of its citizens as

one of the immutable facts of life, no more subject to debate than, say, the sun's rising in the east. Actually, the argument for this point of view suggests that the national state was a relatively novel institution, replacing a feudal system in which differences of class, faith, guild, and estate had, on occasion, mattered far more than national dividing lines. The dangers already inherent in the sovereign state, which assumed most of its present characteristics in the age of absolutism of the seventeenth century, increased in the eighteenth and nineteenth centuries. For it was then that the people, as a whole, came of age politically, and the state was identified not primarily with its monarch but with the entire body politic. It was then, too, that nationalism tended to turn into a faith, replacing previous emotional, and sometimes formal, allegiances now dead.

An aspect of things that made this development especially explosive was that the limited kind of warfare that had characterized past ages was becoming a nostalgic memory—partly because of the advances of technology, but in even larger part, because it was no longer a case of Florence fighting Venice or of Tours having it out with Angoulême. Instead, it was one nation against another: all of France against all of Italy, with the concomitant release of hatreds and energies that had no equivalent in either the civic rivalries of the middle ages and the Renaissance, or in the comparatively civilized cabinet wars of the age of absolutism. National passions, organized or spontaneous, had entered the scene.

Even where these could be contained, something else that was very basic made for great peril. It was the permanent possibility of conflict between nations whose sovereignty was unrestricted. The sovereign state, that law unto itself, faced other sovereign states, and was, considering the propensities of independent entities, as likely as not to come into conflict with them. Yet there existed no organization that could intercede if violence should result from the pursuit of conflicting national interests. There was no higher, supranational authority that could be relied upon to arbitrate between nations bent on mutual destruction.

Where the beginnings of such an authority did exist, its powers were too circumscribed to be effective. The International Court of Arbitration at the Hague could act only if each one of the nations involved in some specific argument voluntarily agreed to submit the case to the Court's jurisdiction, and even then, the Court had no police powers with which to enforce its ruling. (This, incidentally, is a situation that continues unchanged to our day. The Court has changed its name, and been made a part of the United Nations, but its authority is precisely as limited as it was in the years preceding Sarajevo.) What Europe offered, in the phrase of G. Lowes Dickinson, British Liberal and pacifist, was the spectacle of "international anarchy." The national state, unchecked as it was in the exercise of its sovereign power, except for self-restraint born of wisdom or fear, was set on the road to disaster. Trouble, if we accept this interpretation of events, lay deep indeed.

• *Poisonous Medicine? The Alliance System*   What made the risks of international life even more terrifying was the system of alliances that had evolved by 1914. To a majority of powers, the answer to the international anarchy lay not in devising means to diminish national sovereignty, but in finding as many allies as they possibly could among the existing nation states. Faced as they felt they were by "reality," adding to their diplomatic strength by means of casting the widest conceivable net of alliances seemed very much preferable to waiting for Utopia. But should not Europe's statesmen have remembered Molière's words, from *Le Malade Imaginaire,* that "most men die of their medicines, not of their diseases"? Three major, and quite demonstrable, reasons would have seemed to indicate that in this case at least, the cure was worse than the disease.

One was that Europe, after 1907 at the latest, was divided into two hostile camps: the Triple Alliance of Germany, Austria-Hungary, and Italy versus the Triple *Entente* of France, Russia, and Great Britain. Europe's six, then, had chosen sides years before any actual outbreak of hostilities, and in the process had decreased, and perhaps even destroyed, the space for diplomatic maneuvering that was (and is) essential for the preservation of peace.

The second and related point was that under the alliance system, as it then stood, minor powers were in a position to make very major decisions. Some rash action on the part of little Serbia could involve giant Russia in the consequences. Russia, in turn, might involve France. Or Austria-Hungary, with its entanglements in Southeastern Europe, could compel Germany to go to war over issues that were of no imaginable, or certainly of no direct, concern to Berlin. In short, any crisis, no matter how trivial by any reasonable and objective standards, carried the seeds of catastrophe. Given the facts of the alliance system, an offense to any one European nation might ultimately draw in that nation's ally, and then that ally's ally, or allies. The tail could wag a whole pack of dogs.

The third charge, and it is still a related one, was that nations at times were tempted to play a more reckless diplomatic game than they would have under different circumstances. Had they stood alone, their relative weakness might have served them as a continual reminder of the need for compromise and caution, but as it was, they could feel confident that their alliances would shield them from the worst results of their actions. Thus Russian ambitions in the Balkans, for instance, had been rather effectively held in check during an earlier period by the opposition of a number of other powers. But was it not natural that Russia, after the conclusion of the accords with Britain and France, should be inclined to pursue a much less circumspect policy, since in the event of a collision with Austria, or even with Austria plus Germany, St. Petersburg could count on the support of London and Paris? Thus Austria, for years, had been reluctant to pursue too irreconcilable a policy vis-à-vis Serbia. But, in 1909, as the Austro-German alliance hardened, the chief of the German general staff let his Austrian colleague know that if Austria should ever be compelled to march on Belgrade, and if Russia in such an event should come to Serbia's aid, Germany would be certain to go to war against Russia. It was a promise that Bismarck, with his far more skeptical view of alliances had never been willing to make; the idea that Austria might be encouraged to provoke Russia had terrified him. But now that Bismarck was dead and Austria could count on Germany's unquestioned aid, was it really very astonishing that she would act with such intransigence toward Belgrade in 1914?

This then, if we follow this particular argument, was the mood which the alliance system brought to Europe. And it brought it to a continent that was rent by national rivalries which had few precedents in past history.

• *Conflict Overseas: Imperialism* One such rivalry, or rather series of rivalries, took place overseas. The two-score years before Sarajevo were years of all but unparalleled imperialist activity. Not that imperialism was a new fact of European life. The practice, if not the term, had been been quite as familiar to Ferdinand and Isabella as to Benjamin Disraeli. But imperialism seemed to have run its course. During the first three quarters of the nineteenth century, the powers of Europe were showing relatively little interest in acquiring any new territory beyond the confines of the continent. There was a good deal of economic imperialism, particularly on the part of Britain and France—in Latin America, in North Africa, in the Near East—but the outright acquisition of colonies tended to be regarded as an annoyance rather than an asset. The secession of the American colonies had been an object lesson to bear in mind.

In the 1870s, however, the attitude changed and changed abruptly. The powers were once again moving into Africa and Asia, and doing so with such energy and speed that by the time of Italy's Tripolitanian venture, the race was all but over. The end of Europe's overseas frontier had been reached. In the process, there had been acquired vast tracts of land and millions of new subjects. Africa, still largely uncharted in the 1880s, a generation later not only had some excellent maps, but roads and buildings, and hosts of white settlers as well.

The leader in the race was England, although other powers followed very closely. Nevertheless, it was the British who showed just how effectively one of the oldest of colonial powers could meet new opportunities, as they expanded into India, China, Persia, Egypt, the Southern part of Africa, until by 1914, one fifth of the world's land and one fourth of the world's population were under the rule of Britain—the world's largest Empire since Imperial Rome. Then there was France, her gains particularly impressive for a country that, in the wars of the eighteenth century, had lost most of the vast colonial holdings accumulated in the period between Henri IV and Louis XIV. The Third Republic now did as well as any Bourbon monarch ever had, establishing protectorates over Tunisia and Morocco and colonies in Western and Equatorial Africa, and taking control of Indo-China and Madagascar, of Tahiti and a number of other similarly tempting Pacific islands. It was a vast empire, and one whose population easily outnumbered that of the mother-country.

Then there were the powers new, or relatively new, to the colonial game: Germany, Italy, Belgium. In Germany's case, Bismarck's restraint was wearing off. Colonies, he had said, reminded him of the splendid furs some im-

poverished Polish noblemen wore with no shirt under-
neath. His successors felt differently about the matter.
What they wanted were furs, not metaphors, and in their
search they moved into East and Southwest Africa, farther
north into Togoland and the Cameroons, and onto some
Pacific islands as well. Italy, too, whose territory had only
recently provided the scene for other nations' expansionist ambitions, turned from pursued into pursuer. The flag
of Italy went up over Eritrea and the Somaliland, although an attempt to conquer the country bordering both,
Abyssinia, ended in failure. At the battle of Adowa in
1896, the Abyssinians supplied the exception that proved
the rule and startled the world with the news that Africans
had beaten Europeans. But the Italians, as we saw, were
to find another and happily feebler opponent in Turkey,
and manage to incorporate Tripoli into their new empire.
Belgium did even better as she acquired by purchase,
rather than by battle, Congolese territory seventy-five
times the size of Belgium proper—territory, moreover, that
was appreciably richer in resources than Tripoli.

Finally, there were the two powers that, while either
non-European or partly European only, still were very
much part of the imperialist movement. One was the
United States, which in this period annexed Hawaii, the
Philippines, Cuba, Puerto Rico, and portions of Samoa,
and made its presence felt on the Chinese mainland. The
other power was Russia, whose imperialism largely followed the pre-1898 American pattern of expansion not so
much overseas, as on her own continent. Like America's,
Russia's aims were grand indeed. Russia was moving in
the direction of the Middle East, or more specifically, toward Persia and Afghanistan, and toward the Far East,
into Siberia, Korea, and the coastal regions of China.

In was, in sum, an unprecedented epoch of expansion.
Of all the major powers, Austria-Hungary alone kept
aloof, while Spain and Turkey, through lack of strength
but not of desire, lost ground instead of gaining it.

What, however, was the connection between imperialism and war? The answer is that there were impressive arguments for maintaining that imperialism affected the policies of the European powers in several obvious, and ultimately disastrous, ways. There was, for instance, the new mood of violence that it helped to create. If ever one had daily proof of how might made right, imperialism provided it. Sweet were the uses of brute force: they had made the Queen of England Empress of India and created a new France beyond the seas. And it was violence that took place against the background of an often drab, dull, and tedious industrial society, thus making colonial wars seem all the more exciting and colorful.

As the great British historian and long-time Liberal member of Parliament, G. P. Gooch, wrote in 1902: "When we read on the bills: 'Boers sabred by moonlight,' we are supplied by a novel and striking image, which for a time relieves the monotony of life. The Romans clamored for *'panem et circenses.'* We have changed our religion and two thousand years have slipped by, but the cry is the same today." War, in an age where death was becoming mechanized as never before, was given an air of romance and glamor.

There was also another and even more concrete way in which imperialism could be said to have contributed to the destruction of the European order. It was that colonial ambitions required increased armaments. If one was to conquer the heathen—and be ready for possible trouble with some fellow missionaries as well, more money would have to be voted for arms, and so it was. The means as well as the spirit of violence were increasing. Very large amounts of effort went into the production of machineries of conquest. Very small amounts went into any real consideration of the consequences. In retrospect, we are startled by the recklessness with which the nations of Europe pursued their colonial dreams. In their greed, they appeared to be oblivious to the diplomatic repercus-

sions of their Asian and African adventures. Thus, the
1880s and 1890s offered the almost constant spectacle of
crises between England and Russia over who was to control Persia and Afghanistan. Thus, in the Pacific, Germany,
England, and the United States would allow an inordin-
ate amount of friction to develop between them over the
precise delineation of interests on the island of Samoa;
each nation's honor and survival, if one followed some of
their respective spokesmen, were depending on the number of Polynesian palm trees it controlled. Thus, Germany
and France, early in the new century, would twice go to
the edge of war over the matter of spheres of influence
in Morocco.

Lenin, looking on, thought it all very good news. Imperialism, he later wrote, was the final aberration of
capitalism, the most fateful, perhaps, of capitalism's many
inherent contradictions that would speed its end. How
far from wrong was he, when we add to the sampling of
near-wars the real wars that imperialism caused, from the
Boer War to the Boxer Rebellion to the Russo-Japanese
War of 1904–1905? Now it can be said that these wars
were fairly remote in time and cause from World War I
(an argument to which we will return later). But one
aspect of imperialism that was not remote at all was the
manner in which it poisoned relations between Germany
and England. In the end, it would be the hostility between these two countries that would do as much as anything to transform a Balkan assassination into a world
war.

• *Conflict at Home* DARDANELLES TO ALSACE Before deal-
ing with the Anglo-German problem in any detail, however, it might be wise to cast a brief glance at Europe's
basic trouble spots, *circa* 1914. For there existed some
quite profound areas of friction between Russia and Turkey, between Russia and Austria, and between Germany
and France, in addition to those between Germany and

England. There existed others as well, of course; conflicts of interest are the daily bread of diplomacy. Yet it
was on those four areas that the historians' attention has
rightly concentrated. It was here that most of the explosives accumulated.

Russia's foreign policy, to start with the border region
of Europe, was dominated, as it had been for two centuries, by the desire for access to the open seas and to the
trade routes of the world. Specifically, this meant control of the Straits,.and given the weakness of the Porte,
the goal seemed worthier of pursuit than ever.

There was some irony in this, since by this time, the
Straits were a matter of prestige rather than necessity to
Russia. To quote George Kennan:

The regime of the straits that existed in the period prior to
the war occasioned no difficulties for Russian commerce. And if
one looks at the matter from the military standpoint, one can
only say that this region, barring as it did the passage of foreign warships through the straits, was a positive advantage to
a country which had lost most of its naval strength at Tsushima.[1]

Still, this *was* the aim Russia pursued, and it was a
policy of great inherent risk. St. Petersburg was willing
to take the risk because it had not quite adjusted to
changed conditions; the habits of the past were more compelling than the realities of the present. Besides, even
where the statesmen's vision might be sharp and clear,
there was the problem of Pan-Slav pressure.

Pan-Slavism, like official Russia's desire for the Straits,
does not truly make a great deal of sense when looked at
objectively in the second half of the twentieth century.
To quote George Kennan again: "Membership in the
Slavic branch of the human family is not really, as history has shown, a very important bond. Cultural and

---

[1] George Kennan, "The Price We Paid for War," *The Atlantic*
(October 1964), p. 51.

religious traditions, varying widely among the Slavic peoples, are more important as determinants of national policy, in the long run."[2]

Yet there it was. The actual number of dedicated Pan-Slavs in the Russian diplomatic service was relatively small; still, the sentiment and the pressures were there. No Russian foreign minister could entirely disregard them. And Pan-Slav pressures combined with more traditional Russian foreign policy aims—the line dividing the two was a thin one in any event—placed a heavy burden not only on Russo-Turkish relations, but inevitably on Austro-Russian relations as well. The weakness of Turkey was an open invitation to both Russian and Austrian expansion in the Balkans, since none of the successor states to Turkey were viable enough to be wholly independent. True, statesmanship of a very superior order might have avoided or at least mitigated the resulting friction between the two great nations. If, on the one hand, the Austrians had acted with greater wisdom and restraint in 1908 and not faced the Russians with the choice between public humiliation and war, subsequent history might well have taken a happier course. So it might, on the other hand, if Russia had not involved herself quite so deeply in the affairs of Serbia, for what was at stake there was more than a competition for Balkan spoils. It was a question, rather, of national survival, since Belgrade, with Pan-Serb ideas of its own, posed a clear threat to the very existence of the Habsburg monarchy. But these are speculations. The fact was that both powers possessed foreign ministers of only quite ordinary and human ability and imagination, and that the pre-1914 Balkans provided another perennial trouble spot where crisis seemed normal and stability utopian, and where major powers were willing to take some terrible

---

2 Kennan, p. 51.

risks in the pursuit of gains that, from our vantage point at least, seem wholly out of proportion to the price.

Then, closer to the center, there was the enmity that came between France and Germany. We can dispense with a long discussion of its roots; enough has been said about the conditions of the peace of Frankfurt. No more needs to be added here than to reiterate the fact that the French would not forget Alsace-Lorraine, and that a border region which should have been a bridge became a chasm. One of the reasons, for instance, for General Boulanger's vast popularity in the 1880s, and for his near success in destroying the Third Republic, was his supposed toughness toward the Germans:

> See him over there, he smiles as he goes by
> He has just set free Lorraine and all Alsace!

He had done nothing of the kind, nor did the duly constituted governments of France have the power to correct Frankfurt by diplomatic means. The Germans, for their part did not have the wisdom to do so, and so an unjust peace remained to divide two nations whose enmity was anything but eternal.

• THE SOURCES OF ANGLO-GERMAN FRICTION   The Germans did not even possess enough good sense to avoid policies that were bound to create friction with a nation from which no victor's peace kept them apart, that is, with Great Britain.

The causes, on the German side, went beyond any of the specific points at issue. Germany, under Wilhelm II, wished to be a great power. Why not, one might say. For Germany, exuberant in her new-found unity, possessed the population, the military strength, the industrial capacity, the vital energy, that go into the making of a great power. Why not, then? Mainly because Bismarck was gone and the conduct of Germany's foreign affairs rested in hands less steady than his. There was a very great

deal of talk about Germany's might, about how Germany
had been forgotten when the goods of this earth were
distributed, about how Germany must trade the pursuit of
limited objectives for that of *Weltpolitik*. There was
very little clear thought, on the other hand, of what precisely it was that Germany wanted. How really does one
translate *Weltpolitik*? "Global policy" perhaps, a term as
hazy, and at the same time as ominous, as the original.
The translator's difficulties are symptomatic.

The world, not surprisingly, was puzzled and concerned
about the limits of Germany's ambitions. What were the
Germans pursuing? Was it colonies, was it a new emin-
ence on the continent, was it, perhaps, world domination?
We know today that most foreign fears were groundless,
and that no responsible German statesman before 1914
thought in terms of Napoleonic visions. At the time, the
matter was less clear, as the Kaiser's far from subtle at-
tempts to make Germany the equal of Great Britain, and
above all, his ill-considered speeches allowed the impression to flourish that his country was a menace to peace,
security, and a decent society. Many a German could also
see the danger signs. Theodore Fontane, Germany's greatest nineteenth-century novelist, wrote to a friend:

You mention the speeches given by an exalted tongue, in
which so much is said and even more is passed over in
silence. I always lose my temper when I read them . . . .
He has a million soldiers and wants to have a million battleships too. He dreams . . . of humiliating England. Germany
is to be on top, in each and every thing. I rather like all this
—I won't discuss right now whether it is clever or practical—
and I would gladly follow him on his tightrope walk if only I
could see the right sort of chalk under his feet and the proper
balancing staff in his hands. But those are the things he does
not have. What he wants, while it may not be impossible, is
vastly dangerous, and his equipment is wrong and his means
are insufficient.

Not all Germans were as cautious as Fontane. There
had come into existence, simultaneously with Wilhelm's

"New Course," the small but vocal group of Pan-Germans. Their specific aims were even more ill defined and fluid than those of Germany's official spokesmen. They talked of fusing such "Germanic" nations as Holland and Switzerland with the Reich. They dreamt dreams of incorporating, by political or economic union, regions reaching from Brussels to Bucharest into a German-dominated *Mitteleuropa*. They conjured up visions of a truly grand empire in Africa. The precise aims might change; the spirit remained the same. The Pan-Germans forever favored an aggressive and acquisitive approach to foreign policy; they were forever ready to engage in more tightrope walking, secure as they were in the knowledge that there were no ropes like German ropes and no nets like German nets.

The Pan-Germans were a minor group. They were less influential than their Pan-Slav counterparts in Russia, which was fair enough since their program was even more at variance with the world's realities. The largest membership they ever claimed at any given point was well under 25,000, and for the most part it was considerably smaller than that. Yet there existed several factors that made it difficult to deal with them as a mere fringe group. One was that among the members were a fair number of Reichstag deputies; in 1901, their most successful year, thirty-two Reichstag members were Pan-Germans. Another was the volume of the noise they made. A third was that the Kaiser's government, while not making Pan-German aims its own, failed to disassociate itself from their inanities with sufficient force. A fourth was that there were people beyond Germany's frontiers who were quite happy to make sure that the Pan-Germans received a wide hearing.

This applied, in particular, to Great Britain, where any indication of the existence of a German menace found some willing listeners. "It is of course true," noted a senior member of the British foreign office after reading a long dispatch on Pan-German activities, and making quite sure that it would reach the king, "that the Pan-German aspirations to dominion over the Low Countries and over the Adriatic are openly disavowed by all responsible people in Germany. But it would be foolish to doubt that if and when a favourable opportunity occurred for realizing such political aspirations in whole or part, the opportunity would be seized by the German Government with all its wonted energy."

The causes of this sort of suspicion, and of Anglo-German friction in general, were not all on one side of the channel, and on the British side, too, they transcended the individual points at issue. There were, on that side, factors that may make one appreciate why people as sensible and civilized and fond of many things British as Fontane was, wished the Kaiser luck in his policy toward England.

There was, for one thing, an amount of arrogance which exasperated people other than the Germans, too. God, to listen to some British speakers, had left the side of the bigger battalions where He had been in Frederick the Great's days, and permanently joined His cause with Britain's. There was, behind the arrogance, national expansion and power that had few parallels in history. It was, very likely, too much power, since the British Empire covered so much of the globe that just about any move on the part of just about any nation just about anywhere in the world could be considered a menace to either some part of the Empire or to its lines of communication. And the principal challenge to the Empire seemed to come from a nation too newly rich to abide by the rules laid down by British gentlemen, from the Kaiser's Germany. It was a threat to be resisted for moral as well as political reasons; one is back with the matter of arrogance. To quote Raymond Sontag:

Nearly all men, and groups of men, assume that what is good for them is good for the world, and that what is bad for them is bad for the world. Englishmen forgot their history and assumed that their supremacy resulted from the operation of a beneficent moral law. To challenge British supremacy was to challenge moral law. Could the Germans really be so wicked? Roughly speaking, the Conservatives believed that the Germans were capable of this crime; the Liberals were reluctant to entertain such a thought.[3]

That the Conservatives believed it might not have been too tragic, since it was two Liberal ministries, first that of Campbell-Bannerman and then that of Asquith, that held office after 1905. But among those who believed it were some of the permanent officials of the British foreign office as well. A passage written by one of them may serve to indicate their views; it may also illustrate the British attitudes just described. It comes from a memorandum written in 1907, by Sir Eyre Crowe, then the Senior Clerk of the Foreign Office. In a survey of Britain's relations with Germany and France, he had this to say as he came to discuss the matter of naval armaments:

The danger of a general combination against Britain's naval supremacy can in practice only be averted on condition that the national policy of the insular and naval state is so directed as to harmonize with the general desires and ideals common to all mankind. . . . Now the first interest of all countries is the preservation of national independence. It follows that England, more than any other non-insular Power, has a direct and positive interest in the maintenance of the independence of nations, and therefore must be the natural enemy of any country threatening the independence of the others, and the natural protector of the weaker communities. . . . It has been well said that every country, if it had the option, would, of course, prefer for itself the power of supremacy at sea, but that, this choice being excluded, it would rather see England hold that position than any other state.

But that happy state of affairs was in jeopardy, and the source of the threat was plain to Crowe:

---

[3] Raymond J. Sontag, *European Diplomatic History, 1871–1932* (The Century Co., New York, 1933), p. 126.

A German maritime supremacy must be acknowledged to be
incompatible with the existence of the British Empire, and
even if that Empire disappeared, the union of the greatest military with the greatest naval power in one State would compel
the world to combine for the riddance of such an incubus.[4]

Le style c'est l'homme. England, "the natural protector
of the weaker communities." England, the chosen master
of the seas. And why? Because "it has been well said"
that this should be so. Because the possibility of any other
nation's being supreme at sea was "being excluded." But
by whom had it "been said"? By whom was it "being
excluded"? How simple the problems of the world become in the passive tense. German naval supremacy?
(A term which, when properly translated, should read
"increased naval strength," since supremacy, even if the
Germans had aimed at it, which they did not, would have
been decades away.) It "must be acknowledged to be incompatible with the existence of the British Empire"—
after all, that Empire was Germany's "natural enemy."

It was the voice of neither precision nor reason. When
practicing diplomats begin to think of other powers in
terms of natural enemies and of incubi, rather than in
terms of nations with aims, interests, needs, and desires of
their own—some legitimate, some to be resisted—the end
of meaningful discourse is in sight. Perhaps the one
thing that "must be acknowledged" is that Germany was
not the only country to miss a grand old man. Where
was Disraeli? It is hard to visualize him tolerating a
memorandum such as this. Sir Edward Grey, in whose
hands the conduct of British foreign affairs now lay, not
only tolerated it, but recommended it to the attention of
the prime minister. Crowe's observations, he wrote, were
"most valuable. The review of the present situation is

---

4 *British Documents on the Origins of the War, 1898–1914* (London, H. M. Stationary Office, 1928) , III, Appendix A.

both interesting and suggestive, and the connected account of the diplomatic incidents of past years is most helpful as a guide to policy." Grey was a man of great personal probity and attraction, yet, despite his long tenure of office (he served as under secretary for foreign affairs from 1892 to 1895, and as foreign secretary from 1905 to 1916) there was about him something of the air of the gifted amateur. Or, if that is too unkind a term, he strikes one as a statesman under whom expert advisers become makers of policy, and who, rather than shaping events, are all too easily controlled by circumstances.

Men who shape history are admittedly rare. Yet in the absence of genius, on the British as well as on the German side, the Anglo-German dispute continued unresolved. At least three specific problems and a matter of attitude combined to separate the two countries.

There was, in the first place, the economic rivalry between the two powers. The problem was not limited to England and Germany. Trade rivalries existed between a great many European states, and some writers have seen them as one of the truly basic problems aggravating European international relations before 1914. But Anglo-German competition probably was the sharpest of them all. German industrial growth, both in absolute terms and vis-à-vis England, had been phenomenal. In 1870, for instance, Germany had produced 169,000 metric tons of steel as against England's 286,000. In 1910, the figures read 13,698,000 for Germany and 6,374,000 for England. Not all figures were this spectacular; nevertheless, in coal production, Germany increased the yield by 800 percent between 1870 and 1914, England by 200 percent. In similar fashion, the Germans showed by their output of finished goods, particularly of chemicals and of electrical equipment, that while the industrial revolution had come late to their country, it had found a congenial home.

Statistics on exports were keeping pace with those on production. In 1871, for instance, German exports to the United States were well behind those of Great Britain; in 1898, they had nearly caught up; in 1913, they were nearly three times as high. In terms of total exports, Germany, while starting as a poor second indeed, by 1914 had become all but the equal of Britain. It was perfectly true that the world offered enough markets for both these industrial giants, yet the daily competition for sales tended to dramatize the conflict that existed in other fields as well. How was a British member of parliament to react when, during a foreign policy debate, he was to glance at his pencil and see the legend "Made in Germany"?

With trade rivalry went another problem, that of colonial friction. Too often, when the British wished to expand, whether it was in Africa or in the Pacific, there —or so at least it seemed to London—were the Germans, asking for "compensation." Nor would the British very easily forget the gratuitous insult of the Kruger dispatch. With the Germans in Southwest Africa now and in the Cameroons and in East Africa, unbidden and unwanted neighbors to Britain's domains, the memory was likely to remain fresh.

Why this German hunger for colonies, why the break with Bismarckian tradition? In part, German imperialism makes sense, even today. An expanding German industry was in need of markets and, to an even larger degree, in need of raw materials. Yet there is no absolute need to push forward the frontiers of empire in order to assure oneself of a proper supply of kapok from the Cameroons or of cloves from Zanzibar. Less aggressive ways of commerce may work equally well; certainly the Swiss have grown extraordinarily rich without acquiring a single colony. Switzerland, it can be replied, was a small power, Germany a very great one, which could not afford to rely on the good will of her potential enemies for the materials needed to sustain the nation's economy. Still, even when supposedly strategic economic needs are taken into account, there remains an element in Germany's colonial appetite that defies rational explanation. For economic blockades in time of peace tend to be as rare as they are ineffectual; nor was this contingency one that necessarily entered the minds of Germany's leaders. Trade flowed too freely in the years before 1914. It was rather that some Germans were getting intoxicated with their own slogans —of Germany's might, of keeping up with Great Britain, of needing a "place in the sun." Here, as elsewhere, there was much action for action's sake, and little thought about what the limits of Germany's ambitions should be.

Much of this also held true of the third issue that came between Germany and England, the naval race. "Our future," to recall the Kaiser's elegant phrase, "lies on the water." Deeds had followed his words. Under the leadership of Admiral von Tirpitz, Germany's all too energetic Secretary of the Navy from 1897 to 1916, the Germans proceeded to build a navy that was meant to be second only to that of Great Britain.

Some of the motives behind Tirpitz' program were rational enough. Both the expanding German Merchant Marine and the colonies that now flew the German flag deserved the protection of a German fleet. There may also have been an element of sense in the admiral's idea of the "risk navy." Let the German navy, argued Tirtpitz, not aim at supremacy. That was a condition plainly beyond the country's potential. Let Germany's navy, however, be strong enough so that no other and superior naval power would think of attacking it for fear of the losses that such an attack might entail. Let it, in modern parlance, be a deterrent navy. Faced with such a navy, and here came the second, rather less solid part of Tirpitz' argument, the British would surely persuade themselves of the wisdom of reaching some political agreement with Germany.

This, as we know, was a miscalculation. It is not very often that nations can frighten each other into friendship, and the British reaction, not very surprisingly, was that of the clenched fist, and not of the outstretched hand. Not very surprisingly, for what did the Germans really have in mind when they embarked on Tirpitz' program; to what extent had they considered the consequences?

Historically, Germany was a land power with hardly any naval tradition. If one were to look at the new German battleships coming off the yards, one would be struck by how many of them were named after Prussian and German generals—Derfflinger, Moltke, Seydlitz, Goeben, Blücher —since there were simply not enough admirals to lend their names to the christenings. Obviously the British would be vitally concerned, even with people more balanced than Crowe in the foreign office, at the spectacle of Germany, the possessor of Europe's strongest army, setting about the creation of a major navy as well. The direct challenge to Britain's control of the seas quite aside, it was too much power for any one country to hold.

Why, then, did the Germans go ahead, plain though the unfortunate effects of Tirpitz' ambitions on Anglo-German relations were? Why did the Kaiser continue to give the admiral his blessings; how could he tell his Chancellor, as late as the fall of 1913, that "England will come to us not in spite, but because of my Imperial Navy"? There was active here, one suspects, the same element that made the Germans proceed with equal disregard for caution in the colonial sphere: a burning desire to be recognized as Great Britain's equal, and with it, a suspicion that the desire was not likely ever to be fulfilled.

Out of place as the phrase may appear in a diplomatic narrative, there was a deep psychological bond as well as bar between Britain and Germany. What came into play here was a curious love-hate relationship, aggravated by some profound feelings of inferiority on the German side. It could be found in Wilhelm II, who delighted in seeing himself in a British admiral's uniform, who was proud of being half-English (his mother had been Queen Victoria's eldest daughter), who loved reading English books, and who spoke and wrote English with facility and pleasure, and who, at the same time, was worrying whether the British were taking him quite seriously, and behind whose nearly every move lurked fear of being secretly smiled at, of not being truly considered the equal of his cousin Edward and of Eton's best. It could be found among many educated Germans who sensed that no matter how much of Britain's tailoring, country clubs, parliamentary institutions, or orange marmalade they might imitate or import, they would never quite catch up with their cousins beyond the Channel; that they were newly rich but not yet newly wise; that they might be able to buy all the Harris tweed they wished, but that with all the cloth of the Hebrides, they would still lack the proper school tie.

Here is a passage from a German novel, *Peter Moor's Trip to Southwest,* by Gustav Frenssen, that may underline some of this. The book appeared in 1906 and was one of the year's best sellers. Its narrator and title hero is a good and simple fellow who has enlisted in the German marines and at the book's beginning is on his way to German Southwest Africa to fight in a campaign against a native rebellion. As his boat passes the Cliffs of Dover, he chances to overhear the following conversation between an officer in the medical corps and a deck lieutenant:

I heard the lieutenant say: "We sailors have different ideas about the British. . . . We meet them in all the world's ports and we know that they are the most reputable people of them all. There, behind those chalk cliffs, lives the first nation on earth: noble, wise in the ways of the world, brave, united, and rich. But we? For years past, we have had just one of their qualities, bravery. Slowly now, we're gaining one more, wealth. But will we ever gain the rest? There now is the vital question." The words surprised me. But later, the old Africa hands I met also spoke with great respect about the British.[5]

Too often, the respect was not being returned. The "you are to love me!" approach is rarely effective. The

---

[5] Gustav Frenssen, *Peter Moor's Fahrt nach Südwest* (G. Grote, Berlin, 1906) , pp. 14–15.

Germans might have been well advised to drop the matter. How many foreigners, after all, did the British either
love or respect? The Germans rarely paused to consider
that the answer most likely was "none." An occasional
exception was the Kaiser. "He is a thorough Englishman,"
he told Theodore Roosevelt when George V had succeeded Edward VII in 1910, "and hates all foreigners but
I do not mind that as long as he does not hate Germans
more than other foreigners." The insight did not last.
Affection, as it so easily can, turned into hatred. Nor did
the ethnic kinship that existed between the two nations
stay the process. It certainly never acted as a substitute
for missed alliance opportunities. On the contrary, it
had a way of making things worse. Few feuds are as bitter
as family feuds. In the end, when war came in 1914, one
of the most wildly popular poems of the hour would be
a "Song of Hate Against England," by a young and hitherto obscure German poet, Ernst Lissauer. Whom did the
Germans really wish to see humbled? he asked. The
French, whom they had battled in so many wars? No,
not the French. "We love them not, we hate them not."
The Russians, then, the ancient Slav antagonist of the Germans? No again. "We love them not, we hate them not"

> What's the Frenchman to us, or the Russian foe
> We'll meet shot with shot, and blow with blow.

No—"We all have but one foe, England":

> Hate by water and hate by land
> Hate of the head and hate of the hand
> Hate of the hammer and hate of the crown
> Hate of seventy million choking down
> They love as one, they hate as one
> They all have but one foe: England

• *A Matter of Publicity: The Press* The topic of Anglo-
German friction has been stressed at such length because

in a sense it was the ancient nursery rhyme's horseshoe nail. Without it, there might have been no *Entente Cordiale;* without that *Entente,* French support for Russia might have been less resolute; without that support, in turn, Russia might well have acted as a restraining influence on Serbia. For lack of an Anglo-German *détente,* in short, more than one kingdom would be lost.

What aggravated the·points at issue between Germany and England even more was the publicity they received. The Germans not only had a navy, they also had a Navy League, and so did the British, and both these groups sponsored more speeches, books, pamphlets, and letters to the editor than was beneficial to the cause of peace. Nor was there any need to rely on special interest groups to worsen, or at times to create, international disputes; the press, with no particular prodding, did quite well enough at that.

The end of the nineteenth century had seen a new mass literacy, and with it, the creation of a mass-circulation press. The managers of that press were quick to learn that bad news sold more copies than good. "They have ceased to publish the 'Newgate Calendar' and 'The Pirate's Own Book,'" wrote Ralph Waldo Emerson, "since the family newspapers . . . have quite superseded them in the freshness as well as the horror of their records of crime." Emerson was angry, but was he exaggerating that much? "Boers sabred by moonlight." William Randolph Hearst was not the only magnate of the press to discover that crisis and war—stimulated, or even, with great ingenuity, created *ab ovo*—made fine circulation builders. Many a European counterpart to Mr. Hearst would emulate him, exaggerating minor incidents into major crises, presenting another nation's new arms budget as a threat to his readers' survival, or converting the possession of some particular stretch of African jungle into a matter of national honor. The press, in sum, played a substantial part in accentuating international friction, and perhaps even in preparing a mood for war. To quote Sidney B. Fay:

Too often newspapers in all lands were inclined to inflame nationalistic feelings, misrepresent the situation in foreign countries, and suppress factors in favor of peace. . . . There is a vast literature on freedom of the press, censorship of the press, slander and libel, and the professional aspects of journalism, but there is very little sound writing on the relations of the press to governmental control and on its influence in fomenting national hatreds and war.[6]

The role of the press may be an aspect of Europe's pre-1914 troubles that stands in least need of further elaboration and illustration, even though some of the volumes Professor Fay had in mind still remain to be written. We are all quite familiar today with seeing those foreign statesmen whose policies or interests, at some given moment, run counter to ours, pictured as imbeciles, thieves, or megalomaniacs on the editorial pages or in our weekly news magazines. (The latter, perhaps, come closest to the pre-1914 European daily papers in their excess of opinion over fact.) Still, we may draw back a bit as we come across some of the offerings of the pre-war press.

There was the series of reports on Germany in London's mass-circulation *Daily Mail* in 1909, for instance, whose resonance was strong enough to lead to their being reprinted in pamphlet form. "Germany," the reader learned, "is deliberately preparing to destroy the British Empire." Nor was that the extent of Germany's ambition. "All of Europe is to be Teutonised. We are all to be drilled and schooled and uniformed and taxed by Prussian officials, and the Emperor William II is to rule us with a rod of iron." Britain could respond with nothing less than the creation of a larger navy and the introduction of compulsory military service. "Britain alone stands in

6 Sidney B. Fay, *The Origins of the World War* (Crowell-Collier and Macmillan, New York, 1930), I, 47–48.

the way of Germany's realization of world-power and domination."

The attitude was not restricted to that part of the press called "yellow" (as though that epithet was enough to discount its influence). Some years earlier, London's *Saturday Review,* a journal much smaller in circulation and normally far more literate in tone, had carried an article that suggested that in

all parts of the earth, in every pursuit, in commerce, in manufacturing, in exploiting other races, the English and Germans jostle each other. . . . Were every German to be wiped out tomorrow, there is no English trade, no English pursuit that would not immediately expand. Were every Englishman to be wiped out to-morrow, the Germans would gain in proportion. Here is the first great racial struggle of the future: here are two growing nations pressing against each other, man to man all over the world. One or the other has to go; one or the other will go.

The proposed solution was even more simple and radical than that of the *Daily Mail.* Destroy the Germans! *"Germania esse delenda."*

For once, it is easy to sympathize with the Kaiser, who after reading the *Daily Mail* articles said, "They are all mad in England, and people seem to think that I am standing here with my battle axe behind my back ready to fall upon them at any moment." His point might have been even stronger had the German press, in its entirety, been that much more restrained. Instead, some of the notes that *Saturday Review* and *Daily Mail* had sounded were being returned from across the channel. Nor were a number of papers elsewhere on the continent reluctant to join in. There are a few more succinct comments on all this public venom than Humbert Wolfe's lines,

> No one can hope to bribe or twist
> Thank God the British journalist
> But seeing what the man will do
> Unbribed, there's no occasion to.

• *Arms and the Men: War as a Means of Policy*   "Power
without responsibility," Stanley Baldwin is reported to
have said apropos of the press, "the privilege of the har-
lot throughout the centuries." The words were fairly
mild if one considers the damage the press was capable
of inflicting in an age in which war was still an acceptable
means of policy, yet in which the physical nature of warfare was changing beyond the imagination of man.

Here lay another very basic trouble spot of pre-1914
Europe. No matter what was happening in the labora-
tories and on the military proving grounds, war, by implicit agreement among the nations remained the *ultima
ratio regum,* the final argument of kings, the ultimate and
permissible resort in disputes between sovereign states.
In such an atmosphere, as Golo Mann has written:

war, as a concept and an institution, is an important factor
contributing to war itself. Why should not something assume
real shape from time to time which in one's thoughts one considers quite normal, which forms the high point in the life of
nations, which is the standard by which the affairs of state—
in their ranks, values, and morals—tend to be measured.[7]

Yet how much wiser Europe would have been to search
for other standards by which to measure the affairs of
state. For what made the unbroken acceptance of Clause-
witz' celebrated dictum of war as the continuation of
policy by other means especially ominous was the changing nature of those other means. Weapons were becoming
increasingly destructive, and there were too many of them.
The years that reached from the Franco-Prussian War to
Sarajevo were the years of the great arms race between
the powers of Europe. Increased expenditures for armaments were motivated in part by steadily escalating technological improvements, in part by the desire to back
conflicting national ambitions with sufficient force, in

---

[7] Golo Mann, "Gute Vorsätze," *Der Monat* (August 1964), pp.
18–19.

part by the need to keep each nation's military prepared-
ness on a par with that of its potential enemies. No matter what the motives, the speed with which the race was
run had few precedents. Here, then, are some of the basic
statistics on the growth of European armaments in the
period, expressed in terms of per capita expenditures as
translated into dollars:

	1870	1914
Great Britain	$3.54	$8.23
France	2.92	7.07
Russia	1.28	3.44
Italy	1.38	3.16
Germany	1.28	8.19
Austria-Hungary	1.08	3.10

Although Great Britain continued to lead in absolute
terms, by far the greatest single increase was made by
Imperial Germany, and a more detailed breakdown will
indicate that the rate of German armaments accelerated
with particular speed in the years immediately preceding
1914. Yet, while the specific rate of increase might differ,
there was no country which felt that in the pursuit of security and power, it could keep out of the arms race altogether. The irony was that power and security are elusive things, and in the end, no country felt much safer
than before, since the *proportionate* distribution of arms
remained very much what it had been to begin with.
There was, on the contrary, good reason to feel less safe,
since the line between defensive armaments and the readiness for aggression was all but impossible to define.

The nations might have tried to halt the trend had
they been able to visualize the nature of a war fought
with the weapons whose deadliness was being improved
with ingenuity and skill. But most people thought of
war in romantic terms, in terms of gallantry, devotion and
comradeship, all qualities that would turn out to have
comparatively little meaning in the face of the mass-

produced slaughter for which the world was in fact preparing. A few of the experts knew better, but even they
were wrong; for they thought in terms of quick, decisive
campaigns and thus evaded contemplating the full dis-
crepancy between the aims of twentieth-century warfare,
on the one side, and its means, on the other. What no
one foresaw was the kind of murderous yet indecisive
warfare that would open in 1914. The generals played
their war games and speculated, often with considerable
intelligence, about the forms of future warfare, but not
one among then envisaged what would take place between
1914 and 1918.

So the war games went on, and the statesmen did little
to curb them. Here is a final aspect of the question "How
Deep the Trouble?" that should at least be mentioned.
Where were the inspired statesmen of early twentieth
century Europe? Where were the men of power whose
overriding desire was peace, and whose abilities matched
their motives? They were dead. The nineteenth century
had known them—Talleyrand and Metternich, Bismarck
and Disraeli. The twentieth could only honor their
memory.

• *But How Deep the Trouble? Some Conclusions* A
formidable indictment, it seems. The national state and
the alliance system, conflict overseas and conflict at home,
a growing arsenal of arms and a press out for blood, an
acceptance of war and a paucity of statesmanship. Was
not a continent that permitted all these conditions to exist
doomed in any event? At first glance, yes. At a second
glance, we may begin to wonder; and at a third, the
doubts will deepen.

For each and every point of danger mentioned, while
real enough, had quite another side to it, too. The state
system? But that was hardly new, and there neither
was nor is any law stating that national sovereignty
must automatically lead to war. Effectively, suprana-

tional forms of government have either been very rare—
there was but one *Imperium Romanum,* and even in its
case, an occasional fight was necessary to maintain peace—
or quite illusory, such as the Holy Roman Empire, which
in sober truth abounded with war. The national state,
in short, was a reality and had been one for some centuries. Such a state, in the absence of a higher authority,
could go to war; but it was equally free to remain at
peace, and statesmanship, common·sense, self-interest or
fear were all powerful factors pointing to the desirability
of the latter course.

The alliance system, then? Perhaps, if the alliances had
actually been as binding and inflexible as some writers have
made them out to be. But they were not. The British would
consistently refuse a clear-cut promise to come to the assistance of France, let alone of Russia, in case of war. Every
one of the alliances was quite specifically defensive in character, and as the Italians were to show, it was perfectly
possible to change sides with impunity. In fact, instead
of assailing a system that in essence was and is no more
than the common pursuit of common interests (a difficult
ambition to outlaw) might one not rather say that if only
the alliances had been stronger, Europe would have been
less troubled? To give but two specific illustrations, if,
for instance, the Austrians had been certain beyond a
doubt that an attack on Serbia would be an attack on
Russia, or if the Germans had been altogether convinced
that to invade France would, undoubtedly, involve them
in war with England, might not history have taken a happier course? (A matter of speculation? Yes. But it is the
basic assumption on which the western alliance system
since the end of the Second World War has rested.)

What, though, of imperialism? That its effects on
Anglo-German relations were deplorable should need no
further elaboration. However, it should be said that it
made Anglo-Russian and Anglo-French relations fully as
difficult. There was far more colonial rivalry between

Britain and France, for instance, than between France and
Germany—the Germans and the French, after all, had
no Egyptian campaign of 1798 to fight over again—and
the Anglo-Russian wrangling that went on over Persia
alone was every bit as sharp as any Anglo-German conflict of interests in Africa. Yet for all their imperialist
rivalries, England, Russia, and France would ultimately
find an alliance both possible and profitable. That imperialism could accentuate trouble was evident. What was
equally evident, however, was that it could, as the case
of the relationship between the United States and Great
Britain after 1898 showed, bring about the realization
that the interests of two nations were best served by cooperation. Beyond this, one ought to say that the absence
of colonial ambitions was, in at least one instance, a cause
for regret. To quote A. J. P. Taylor, whose insights can
be as perceptive as his fallacies can be mischievous: "All
the Great Powers except Austria-Hungary found a safe
channel for their exuberance in expansion outside Europe.
They stumbled on this solution by chance, without fore-
sight.[8]" If only it had been possible to deflect Austria's
interests from the Balkans to the South Seas, how much
better that would have served the cause of European peace.

What of the more specific conflicts between the nations
of Europe, the quarrels closer to home? Again, one hesi-
tates to say that by themselves they doomed Europe in
1914. For surely one of the common denominators between the various issues that set Russia against Turkey,
Austria against Russia, or France against Germany, was
that none were worth a war. Russia might want the
Straits, and want them badly, but given the opposition of
Britain, France, and Austria, she was quite unwilling to
risk an armed conflict over them. Austria might argue
every inch of the way with Russia over Balkan spheres of

---

[8] A. J. P. Taylor, *The Struggle for Mastery in Europe* (Oxford
University Press, Oxford, 1954), p. 256.

influence, but the choice made was to let the diplomats and not the generals do the battling. France might seize every chance to change the verdict of Frankfurt, but it was every chance short of war. Whatever the period's equivalent of Henry IV's favorite city, it was worth a mass, but not the lives of one's countrymen. Or, to put the matter in another perspective, Russia, in the period that followed the First World War, faced territorial grievances infinitely worse than she, or for that matter, any other European nation confronted before 1914, *without* taking recourse to war to rectify them.

Besides, nothing is forever in diplomatic history. Russia and Austria, for instance, had lived through sustained periods of diplomatic harmony as well as of hostility; few powers had been closer partners than St. Petersburg and Vienna during the quarter century or so after the Napoleonic settlement. Circumstances had changed, but so they might again. There was no reason why alignments should not begin to shift once more, why partnership could not replace rivalry. This applied with equal force to Anglo-German relations. Again, none of the specific instances of friction mentioned were precisely trifling in nature, but neither were they irreparable. Trade rivalry there was, but there was also beginning to be an understanding on the peaceable division of the world's markets, with the British concentrating on trade with the Empire, the Germans on that with continental Europe. Besides, except in Marxist mythology, nations seldom go to war with each other to increase the ratio of their export trade. In theory, this is what should be happening, "war," if we follow the official *History of the Communist Party of the Soviet Union,* "is the inevitable concomitant of capitalism." But in reality, things were rather different. During the Algeciras crisis, for instance, the most determined advocates of a peaceable settlement were the representatives of the French and German coal industry, for they not only dreaded the price of war, they also were very much aware of the advantages which Franco-German co-operation would bring. When the final crisis came, as Bernadotte Schmitt has noted, "the loudest protests against war were made by the businessmen in Germany and Britain, who foresaw clearly what war would do to them."[9]

How much more serious, in the actual event, were naval and colonial rivalries? True, the Germans might have done well to make Falstaff's motto their own. Discretion would have been the better part of valor. But not all was bluster. Germans and Englishmen, as noted, had agreed, by quiet negotiation, rather than by public collision, on the division of the Portuguese colonies. Some overall efforts to limit the naval race, such as that undertaken by Lord Haldane, then Secretary of War, during a mission to Berlin in 1912, ended in failure, but the two nations, by 1914, had managed to reach an informal understanding to construct new battleships at a ratio of Britain's 16 to Germany's 10. There was no reason why more instances of accommodation could not follow—not even the psychological bar between the two nations. A look at some photographs of Edward VII enjoying a state visit plus family outing with his cousin Wilhelm may suggest that more than party manners or the anticipation of a good meal lay behind the smiles and the bonhommie. True, such periods of contentment might alternate with others of utter distemper, but that was hardly a problem that applied to Anglo-German relations alone.

The love-hate relationship, for one, between the United States and Great Britain paralleled it rather closely. It offered the same spectacle of the transaquatic cousins who would now detest and now embrace each other, of the American who would now lionize his British visitor and

---

[9] Bernadotte E. Schmitt, *The Origins of the First World War* (Published for the Historical Association by Routledge and Kegan Paul, London, 1958), p. 5.

now delight in twisting his tail, of the Britisher who would now envy those Americans for their wealth and now think them vulgar for it, of the American who would now make fun of the broad "a" and now join the English-Speaking Union. Yet, there was, in this period, neither war nor the threat of war between these two powers. But that was different, one might say. National interests coincided, so it was easy enough to keep whatever antipathies existed from influencing the conduct of foreign policy. Perhaps so, but to repeat the truism: nothing is forever in diplomatic history. There was no immutable rule which stated that Britain and Germany could never again inhabit a world in which their interests would once more run parallel. Psychological barriers, by themselves, certainly were not deep enough to prevent such a state of affairs, if only for the simple reason that if a good many Britishers still tended to dislike the Germans, there were others who detested the French or Russians even more.

What about the press and its role, then? The case here is strong. Who would not wish that editors and publishers had never discovered the charms that lay in fomenting international trouble. Yet there existed a mass audience avid for precisely this sort of entertainment. To have asked the owners of the press to refrain from supplying what their readers wanted—and what their own prejudices as often as not made them want as well—would have been expecting a great deal more wisdom and self-restraint than is given to the vast majority of men. Nor could the press, by itself, quite start a war. "Remember the Maine" was a one-time coup, never to be repeated. That the press lent a special element of danger to the ordinary conduct of diplomacy was true, yet when all the evidence is considered, the influence of the press was sustantially smaller than its own spokesmen throught. The final decisions continued to remain with the prime minister and not the night editor.

But were not chauvinistic editorials twice as perilous

in a society that continued to accept war as a means of policy, that daily added to its arsenal of arms, and that had not enough statesmen of vision to keep the warmakers in check? Again, one wonders. For it was, and is, easy enough to point to the dangers that flow from the acceptance of war; it is rather more difficult to say what might be done to prevent the dangers that were, or are, likely to result from the abandonment of war as a means of policy. Would a nation announcing that it would under no circumstances have recourse to war truly be furthering the cause of peace—its own or that of others? Yet an argument against war as the ultimate resort of kings which fails to suggest what else the king might resort to will have to carry relatively little conviction. On the contrary, in the eyes of both statesmen and public, were not the preparations for war a true insurance against a war's actually taking place? Vickers and Krupp were not really kept as busy as they were turning out guns and shells because the men ordering these arms wished to use them against any live targets; rather each side wished to convince the other of their strength and seriousness of purpose, and hence of the unwiseness of deciding in favor of armed conflict. *Si vis pacem, para bellum.* Deterrence, by many another name, is rather a venerable concept. So is that of leading from strength. To quote Raymond Sontag: "Armed forces were not intended primarily for use in war; they were to bring victory without war by forcing rival states to give way without an armed encounter."[10]

But what if the available statesmanship did not match the weapons of destruction? After all, it takes keen eyesight and nimble feet to sense just where the brink ends and the precipice begins. How could matters have ended well at a time when Bethmann was sitting in Bismarck's chair, and Grey was holding the office once filled by Castlereagh? The answer—at times even rhetorical ques-

---

[10] Raymond Sontag, *European Diplomatic History*, p. 146

tions deserve an answer—was that matters very possibly could have ended well, for not only is genius customarily in short supply, but the statesmen of Europe were, with hardly an exception, if not inspired, at least competent and often quite shrewd men. So were many of the people serving under them, especially the diplomats in the field. As one looks at the dispatches of Paul or Jules Cambon, or of others for whose mention it has been hard to find room in a necessarily concise narrative—Marschall von Bieberstein on the German side, for instance, or Sir George Buchanan on the British—one is tempted to think of the era as at least the silver age of European diplomacy. And these were, again almost without exception, men genuinely committed to the cause of peace. Count Pourtalès, Germany's ambassador to St. Petersburg, openly wept when all had failed and, his hands shaking, he delivered his country's declaration of war to a Russian foreign minister who, in reply, embraced the representative of the power that Russia was now pledged to fight to the finish. Pourtalès' colleagues might do better at controlling their public displays of emotion, but they would feel as he did. The people, when the end came, were jubilant; the statesmen remained sober.

How deep, then, the trouble? Deep, but not fatal. War was possible in 1914—when is it not?—but it was not inevitable. An anatomy of many another year, whether 1874, 1884, 1894, 1904, or 1964, if undertaken as mercilessly as the inquest into 1914 necessarily is, may quite likely uncover troubles fully as profound as those of 1914.

We do not, for obvious reasons, undertake such inquests, but we may say that everything considered war was no more foreordained for 1914 than peace was for 1964. Too much was right with the world of 1914: the nations, on the whole, had learned to live with the differences that divided them; several of the outstanding points at issue between rival powers were being settled or mitigated; and as the changing relationship between

Britain and France, France and Italy, or Russia and Britain had shown, nations that were very dissimilar in temper, ambitions, and historical memory were fully as capable of accommodation as they were of conflict. History is forever in flux. In time, the particular difficulties that beset Europe *circa* 1914 might well have vanished, changed, or looked rather insignificant when placed next to other and newer problems.

The exception and not the rule is 1939. It is rare that a power is truly bent on war, as Hitler's Germany then was. In 1914, that sort of will to war was absent, although error, miscalculation, and sheer accident were very much present. But let us, because they were present, and because the end result was catastrophe, not become too absorbed by a sweeping search for underlying causes. Let us avoid the fallacy of saying that because the First World War's consequences were so momentous, its causes must of necessity have been equally significant. Captain Jenkins claimed to have had an ear cut off by some overly zealous Spanish guards in 1739, and England plunged into a war with Spain that lasted for two years. It was, Frederick the Great later admitted, his youth and "the satisfaction of seeing my name in the newspapers" which had in truth caused him to attack Maria Theresa in 1740 and to begin the long War of the Austrian Succession. Of course, other and deeper causes contributed to the origins of both of these wars, but so did these immediate reasons. Of course, there were many explosives about in early twentieth-century Europe—there seldom are not—but it still took a fire to light them, and certain quite unpredictable winds to fan the flames. We need, therefore, if we are to understand the war's origins, to turn to its direct source, the assassination of Archduke Franz Ferdinand of Austria-Este, and to the events that followed it.

4 Catastrophe:
Sarajevo, the July Crisis,
and the Outbreak of War

• *The Shots of June:* THE PREPARATIONS More than half
a century after the double murder of Sarajevo, a fair
number of essential facts surrounding the crime's origins and authorship still remain in doubt. Some of the
participants have told stories in which they have freely
mingled truth with fiction. Others have kept entirely
silent. Others yet have been silenced. The account that
follows can therefore claim no more than that it is based
on the testimony of the more credible among the surviv-
ing witnesses, and that it appears to be the most likely
among several possible versions. But with these reservations in mind, as we try to reconstruct the story, it would
seem that at some point between late 1913 and early 1914,
Dragutin Dimitrijević, a lieutenant colonel in the Royal
Serbian Army, decided that he wished Franz Ferdinand,
heir apparent to the throne of Austria-Hungary, to die.

Dimitrijević was an interesting person. The official
position he held was that of chief of intelligence of the
Serbian army. Among the unofficial activities to which he
devoted himself were the affairs of a secret society named
Union or Death, an organization more popularly known,
to the extent that it was known, as the Black Hand. The

aim of the Black Hand, as of several other groups working
in harmony or in competition with it, was the creation of
a Greater Serbia, to include Bosnia-Herzegovina to the
west, and Macedonia to the southeast. Toward this end,
the Black Hand sponsored a substantial amount of propaganda and subversion in those regions. Toward this end,
too, Dimitrijević resolved on the death of Franz Ferdinand.

Archduke Franz Ferdinand of Austria-Este was heir to
a throne whose occupant, the Emperor Franz Joseph, was
eighty-four years old and frail. Franz Ferdinand's acces-
sion to power might spell the end of Dimitrijević's hopes;
too much had been reported about the Archduke's political plans and ideas. The precise shape these plans
would have taken must of necessity remain conjectural,
but it would seem that in one form or another, Franz
Ferdinand was ready to grant some notable concessions
to the empire's Slavs. One scheme discussed would have
provided for the establishment of Trialism, with the al-
lotment of a role to the Slavs comparable to that played
by the Germans and Magyars in the monarchy. Another
involved the possible introduction of a more federal system along American or Swiss lines. Whatever their specific shape, the archduke's projected reforms had to be
anathema to the Black Hand. The last thing that organization wished to see in Bosnia was happy Slavs. The foun-
dation of its work was a discontented minority.

Dimitrijević, then, had a fairly compelling motive for
murder. He also had the opportunity. Franz Ferdinand,
he learned, would be coming to Bosnia in June 1914 to
attend some army maneuvers, at whose conclusion he
would pay a state visit to the Bosnian capital of Sarajevo. In addition to motive and opportunity Dimitrijević
had the means: a group of three young nationalist Bos-
nians resident in Belgrade, Trifko Grabež, Nedjeljko Čabrinović, and Gavrilo Princip, who were willing to kill and,
if caught, take the consequences. After first being trained
by the Black Hand in the use of firearms and bombs, the

three were equipped with the requisite weapons (as well as with vials of cyanide, so that they could commit suicide once they had accomplished their mission) and smuggled back across the border into Bosnia, from where they openly traveled to Sarajevo.

Here, on the morning of June 28, 1914, they took up the stations planned for them along the route that the Archduke and his wife Sophie were scheduled to take on their trip through the city. It was a day of particular significance and bitter memories to any Serb, since it marked the anniversary of the fourteenth-century battle of Kossovo, or Blackbirds' Field, against the Turks that had brought an end to Serbian independence and placed the nation under Turkish vassalage. It had not been excessive tact that had guided the Austrians to choose this day of all days for the Archduke's visit. On the other hand, both the assassination and its details had been planned some time before the precise date of the Sarajevo visit was known. It was indignation directed in advance, not any sudden visions of Kossovo producing homicidal impulses too strong to resist, that threatened the Archduke.

The three young men from Belgrade were augmented by a group of four local associates, although "augmented" may be a misleading term, since none of the four matched them in either resolution or courage. They had, one strongly suspects, been placed there mainly in order to give the crime the flavor of a more home-grown affair.

Not one of the seven, by the way, might have been able to take up his post that morning had a political decision made earlier in Belgrade gone just a bit differently. The facts—to the extent, again, that any "fact" about Sarajevo can truly be asserted—were these: some time in May, Nikola Pašić, Serbia's prime minister, learned about Dimitrijević's plot. This knowledge confronted him with a truly unenviable choice. If he were to tell the Austrians nothing and allow the assassination to proceed, he risked incurring the gravest of diplomatic crises and quite pos-

sibly war. If, on the other hand, he were to warn Vienna
in an effort to prevent the plot from succeeding, he would
in so doing have to admit just what sort of anti-
Austrian activities had been tolerated on Serbian soil.
In fact, he would also risk incurring the open enmity of
the Black Hand at a time when his government's relations with that organization happened to be strained
enough as it was. A possible third choice, the dismissal of
Dimitrijević and the suppression of the Black Hand, apparently never struck Pašić as at all realistic, an estimate
in which he very probably was right.

The compromise Pašić chose in the end, considering the
dilemma that he faced, was as bad as it was comprehensible. He instructed the Serbian envoy in Vienna to
look up the Austrian minister in charge of Bosnian affairs and suggest to him, in very general terms, that he
consider a cancellation of the archducal visit. This, early
in June, was what the envoy proceeded to do. Given the
discontent among Bosnia's Serbs, he said, might it not be
wiser to have the maneuvers take place in some other province of the Empire and to have Franz Ferdinand refrain
from visiting Sarajevo. No, no, said his kindly and guile-
less Austrian host, there was no need to worry; according
to his information, things had been very peaceful in
Bosnia recently. This ended the conversation. The envoy's message had been so lacking in specific information,
and the minister hence so unmoved by it (although he
did try to humor his visitor by saying, as he showed him
to the door, "Let us hope nothing does happen") that
neither Franz Ferdinand nor the police were as much as
informed of the envoy's call. Nor did Belgrade, even
though aware of what had, or rather had not, taken
place, ever revert to the matter.

That the Austrians, then, were not even aware of the
fact that they had been warned was perfectly understandable. What was less so was that the security precautions
taken in Sarajevo during Franz Ferdinand's visit were at

best routine, and at worst very careless. Of the thousands
of troops in the area for maneuvers, none were used to
guard the streets. Instead, all security arrangements were
left in the hands of the local police, who numbered no
more than a hundred and twenty in all. This included
uniformed police and plainclothes detectives, and while
perhaps the force was not inordinately incompetent, they
were certainly no more efficient than an average provincial
police force—whether in Sarajevo, Bosnia or in Dallas,
Texas—is likely to be.

• SARAJEVO, JUNE 28   Even so, what followed that fateful
Sunday, June 28, 1914, was not foreordained. The day's
program for Franz Ferdinand and his party comprised
first a reception at the city hall, followed by a visit to
the local museum, then lunch at the governor's residence,
and after that, the departure for Vienna. At about 10
A.M., the visitors set out on their way to the city hall. They
were traveling in a number of open touring cars, with
Franz Ferdinand, his wife Sophie, and the governor of
Bosnia, General Potiorek, riding in the second car. They
passed the first conspirator, one of the locally recruited
boys, who in a flash decided that dearly as he wished to
see Franz Ferdinand dead, he rather fancied the idea of
staying alive himself; hence he did absolutely nothing to
disturb that arrangement. A minute or so later, the
cavalcade passed the second conspirator. He was Nedjeljko
Čabrinović, one of the Belgrade-trained group. Čabrinović
drew his bomb from his pocket, struck its percussion cap
against a lantern post, took careful aim at Franz Ferdinand's general's helmet with its green panache, and let go.
    Two things happened next. One was that the driver of
the archduke's car, seeing the black object hurtling at
him, instinctively pressed his foot down on the accelerator,
so that, with the car speeding forward, the bomb did not
directly strike its intended victim. The other was that
Franz Ferdinand, having also caught sight of Čabrinović's

missile, raised his hand to protect his wife. With this motion, he chanced to deflect the bomb, which fell into the
street directly behind his car. There it exploded, injur-
ing a number of spectators lightly and giving the governor's aide, riding in the next car, a head wound that
looked serious enough to require his being taken to the
hospital.

The plot, so painstakingly prepared by Dimitrijević
and his friends, appeared to have failed. Within minutes,
Čabrinović was under arrest. The cars went on their way
again, and not one of the remaining five conspirators that
they passed had either the courage or the presence of
mind to raise a hand against Franz Ferdinand.

At the city hall, once the formal reception was over
("All the citizens of the capital city of Sarajevo," said
the mayor solemnly as his archducal guest fumed, "find
that their souls are filled with happiness, and they most
enthusiastically greet your Highnesses' most illustrious
visit with the most cordial of welcomes") Franz Ferdinand,
his aides, and the representatives of the local authorities
went into a quick conference to decide how best to alter
the remaining program for the day. One narrow escape
was quite enough; there was no need even for an officer
and a Habsburg to take additional risks.

Hurriedly, they considered, and rejected, three suggestions that in the event would very likely have saved the
archduke's life and prevented a world war. One was to
cancel the museum visit and to drive directly to the governor's residence. Another was that to be even safer, they
drive back, at high speed, to Franz Ferdinand's hotel outside Sarajevo. Franz Ferdinand rejected both. He did
not mind making some concessions for the sake of security, but he felt that he must visit Potiorek's wounded aide
at the hospital before leaving Sarajevo. The next suggestion someone then put forward was to wait at the city
hall until two companies of troops could be brought into
town from the maneuver area and the streets cleared of

spectators. This one was rejected by the governor. The troops, said Potiorek, were not in proper uniform to be lining the streets.

Still, the arrangements finally agreed on were sensible enough. The group would avoid the narrow side streets of the original route and instead drive first to the hospital by way of Sarajevo's main avenue, the Appel Quay, and then continue on to the museum by an equally unscheduled route. The plan might well have worked had it not been for two factors. One was that at the time the discussion was going on at the city hall, Princip crossed from the sun-drenched river side of the Appel Quay where he had been standing, to the shaded side of the avenue and strolled a few steps down Franz Joseph Street, a shopping street that led off the Quay. The second was that no one informed the driver of Franz Ferdinand's car about the changed plans.

What happened next was this: Instead of driving straight down the Appel Quay, the car carrying Franz Ferdinand, his wife, and the governor turned into Franz Joseph Street, precisely as the chauffeur had originally been instructed to do. As it did so, Potiorek, realizing the error, leaned forward and called, "What is this? This is the wrong way! We're supposed to take the Appel Quay!"

The driver (a general's orders are a general's orders) put his foot on the brakes and began to back up. The maneuver put the car in a straight line with Princip. Princip stepped forward, drew his gun, and from a distance of not more than five feet, fired twice. No amount of planning could have provided him with a better target. One bullet pierced Franz Ferdinand's neck, while the other entered Sophie's abdomen.

The Duchess, not wholly aware perhaps in the first second or so of what had been taking place, but seeing blood spurt from her husband's mouth, called, "For heaven's sake! What happened to you?" and slipped from her seat, her face falling between the Archduke's knees.

Franz Ferdinand, turning to his wife despite the bullet in his neck, said "Sophie dear! Sophie dear! Don't die! Stay alive for our children!" Fifteen minutes later, both were dead.

• *The Echo in Vienna* Within hours, extra editions of the Viennese papers carried the story from Sarajevo. The news caused more political anger than personal sorrow. Franz Ferdinand had not been a widely beloved man— "nothing in his life became him like the leaving it"— but the political implications were obviously ominous. Initial information about the assassins might be scarce, but what was known was that they were ethnic Serbs, and they had committed their act in politically restive Bosnia with its border toward Serbia, facts quite sufficient to throw strong suspicions on Belgrade. What was to be done now?

The men in charge of conducting the policies of Austria-Hungary were not sure. They were not exactly unaccustomed to Serbian-supported acts of terror, propaganda, and sabotage on Austrian soil, but this brazen act was something new, provided that the Serbian government could in fact demonstrably be connected with the two murders. Could it? Was the crime different in nature from previous provocations? Should Austria-Hungary now resort to arms, as some among the military had repeatedly suggested ever since the Annexation Crisis, even though Franz Ferdinand, on that and subsequent occasions, had consistently argued against war? The government did not quite know. Hence they would explore two matters first. One was Germany's attitude. Would Vienna be able to count on Berlin in case an Austro-Serbian conflict widened into general war, as well it might, since Russia could conceivably come to Serbia's aid? The other was the question of evidence. To pursue it, a senior official of the foreign ministry, Friedrich von Wiesner, was charged with an investigation of the assassination. Would he ascertain what proof, not suspicion but proof, there was to connect the assassins with Belgrade.

By themselves, these reasons for delay were far from bad. Austria, unaided, was in no position to win a war against a Russo-Serbian coalition. Even against Serbia alone, it now turned out, the army was unprepared to strike quickly; mobilization would require at least two weeks. Also, it would be of 'considerable advantage to adduce proof of Belgrade's culpability before making the first overt move. (The United States, in 1962, waited very patiently until it could substantiate its charges against the Soviet Union before imposing its blockade on Cuba.) Yet in a way, a discussion of the merits of Vienna's motives for procrastination is irrelevant, for the delay, no matter how defensible its reasons, turned out to be a disaster. In retrospect, it is obvious that if Austria had acted forcefully and decisively against Serbia on June 29, when the impact of the double murder was at its sharpest, the sympathies of the world would have been with the bereaved Dual Monarchy, and the very worst that might have happened would have been a limited war between Austria-Hungary and Serbia. Nor was it quite that hard to see at the time that this should be so. Had the Austrian foreign ministry been in better hands, this very likely would have been the course followed.

• *Germany's Blank Check* (*July 5–6*) A week after the murder, the Austrians had the answer to their first question. On Sunday, July 5, a special emissary sent by the Austro-Hungarian foreign minister, Count Leopold von Berchtold, arrived in Berlin, bearing a personal letter from Franz Joseph to William II. The Dual Monarchy, read the letter, (which was obviously inspired by Berchtold rather than by the privately much more reluctant Emperor) could withstand "the Pan-Slav flood" only if "Serbia's role as a power factor in the Balkans is ended." One would have to aim at the "isolation and diminution of Serbia." What would Germany's position be if Austria now followed such a course?

That morning the Austrian ambassador presented the letter to William at the New Palace in Potsdam. The Kaiser at first avoided comment. Then, after a sociable lunch with his visitor, he abandoned his reserve. Would the ambassador tell his sovereign that even in the event of "some serious European complications," Austria-Hungary could rely on "Germany's full support." If Russia, to put the matter more specifically, should come to the aid of Serbia, then Germany would aid Austria. In fact, asked William II, why not strike against Belgrade right now? As matters stood, the Russians were "hardly ready for war and would certainly think very carefully before resorting to arms."

In the afternoon, the German Chancellor, Theobald von Bethmann Hollweg, who had joined the others at the New Palace, confirmed his monarch's promise, and the ambassador was able to inform Berchtold of Germany's "blank check." The phrase was all too apt. The Austrians were free to fill in the amount on a form that the Germans had cosigned in advance.

There are several quite plausible explanations for this piece of German folly. The Emperor apparently thought that the Austrians would now proceed to act without further delay, and that, given the merits of their case against Serbia and Russia's relative unreadiness for war, whatever fighting there might be would be confined to Austria and Serbia. The German foreign minister, a less sanguine man, was not available for comment and counsel that weekend; he had recently gotten married and was on his honeymoon in Switzerland. The Chancellor, who was there, was full of forebodings but felt that Germany had no alternative but to say Yes to the Austrians. "It is our old dilemma in any Austrian Balkan action," he grumbled to an aide a day later. "If we encourage them, they say that we pushed them into it. If we dissuade them, they say that we abandoned them." And everything considered, dissuasion was the worse evil, for "in that case, they will draw close to the Western powers, whose arms are open, and we will lose our last powerful ally."

These reasons deserve to be mentioned; it was neither utter blindness nor invincible malevolence that made the Germans act as they did. Yet in a sense, they are as irrelevant as are the explanations for Austria's procrastination. Half a century after the event, we are still staggered by the ineptitude of the German response. For the risk— not the intent, but the risk—was the destruction of the European peace, and with it, of Imperial Germany itself. That risk was out of all proportion to the possible gain, and it did not take hindsight to know this. Bethmann's aide, after recording the words just cited, went on to note in his diary: "An action against Serbia could lead to a world war. The Chancellor expects that such a war, no matter how it might end, will revolutionize all that exists."

Twenty-five years before that, Bismarck had written to his king: "Only some complications between Austria and Russia could involve Germany in a war with Russia. Since the cost of such a war, even under the most favorable of circumstances, would be unacceptable for Germany, we must endeavor to do what we can to prevent the Austrian war."

Bethmann had done less than that. The ultimate decision now lay with Austria.

• *"There Is Nothing to Indicate. . . .": The Wiesner Investigation (July 13)* At the foreign ministry in Vienna, Berchtold was delighted with the German promise. It was now or never, he thought, that the Habsburg monarchy should move against Serbia. Twenty-four hours later, however, there arose a formidable obstacle to his plans. In a council of ministers held on July 7, Count Stephan Tisza, prime minister of the Hungarian half of

the monarchy, sharply opposed war or any course of diplomatic action that might lead to war with Serbia.

Tisza was a devout Calvinist who abhorred the use of
force. "War," he wrote in a family letter in August 1914,
"even if victorious, is terrible. To my soul, every war
means misery, anguish, devastation, the shedding of innocent blood. . . ." Tisza was also a working Magyar
politician who had no interest at all in "diminishing"
Serbia. Hungary had enough dissatisfied minorities within
its borders; he wished to acquire no more. It would be
a grave mistake, he told the council of ministers, to force
the issue with Serbia. A European war would be a "terrible calamity." And by the way, he would like to in-
quire where the Sarajevo police had been that bloody
Sunday. It surely was "an unspeakable state of affairs if
six or seven characters armed with bombs and guns could
line the route of the murdered Heir to the Throne and
not have the police observe or remove a single one of
them."

Berchtold and his friends labored hard to change Tisza's
attitude. An investigation of the Sarajevo police would
have to wait, they said. What mattered now was to strike
against Serbia; any "policy of hesitation or weakness"
might lose Austria-Hungary the future support of Germany. (The irony was unconscious, but both the Germans
and the Austrians were talking themselves into risking
their own destruction for fear of losing one another as an
ally.) In the end, Tisza gave in, though only on condition
that the monarchy would not annex "an inch of Serbian
territory." The concession was readily granted, since it
was meant to be broken from the moment it was made.

It had taken a week to persuade Tisza. Meanwhile,
more precious time had been lost. World opinion was
recovering from the initial shock of the double murder.

Perhaps it might be possible to revive some of the lost
indignation by providing new details about the crime and,
above all, by uncovering some clear evidence that would

connect official Serbia with the plot. The person entrusted with that task had been Friedrich von Wiesner of the Austrian foreign ministry. To follow his investigation, we need to retrace our steps to June 28 for a moment.

Immediately after Čabrinović's attempted, and Princip's successful attack, the two young men had followed the instructions they had received in Belgrade and attempted to commit suicide. It was Colonel Dimitrijević's only really reliable assurance that, if arrested, they would not talk. However, no murder planned by remote control can be entirely perfect, and the cyanide capsules that Čabrinović and Princip managed to swallow as they were being arrested and led to the police station caused them some modest pain and discomfort, but did not prove fatal. For reasons unknown then, and likely to remain unknown in the future, the poison they had been given was defective.

The Sarajevo police, then, had Princip and Čabrinović safely in custody; and in the days that followed, nearly all of the local fellow conspirators were arrested—some because they were routine suspects, others because one of Princip's friends talked too much. The authorities might now have found the evidence linking the assassins to Colonel Dimitrijević, had it not been for the extraordinary skill with which Princip and his associates fended off the questions they were asked about Belgrade, a skill impressive even in the face of a certain lack of imagination with which the investigating judge was handling their interrogation.

Even so, the young men could not hide the fact that Princip and Čabrinović had been recent visitors to Belgrade, nor could they very well deny that the bombs used had been of Serbian manufacture. (The guns were Belgian army issue.) In addition, the names of two men who had aided the assassins in Belgrade finally emerged from the questioning. They were those of Milan Ciganović, a Serbian railroad employee, and of Voja Tankosić, a major in the Serbian army. But what the Sarajevo authorities did not discover in this connection was as important as what they did. They never learned that Tankosić was Colonel Dimitrijević's Black Hand aide; in fact, they were to remain wholly unaware of the existence of the colonel and his organization.

On July 10, von Wiesner arrived in Bosnia. He had studied all the material available to him in Vienna and found it of little profit. He now spent day and night in Sarajevo conferring with the authorities and going over the files they had been accumulating. On the morning of July 13, after four hours of sleep, Wiesner drafted the dispatch for which Vienna had been waiting.

The body of his report mentioned the links he had been able to establish between the crime and Belgrade: the bombs, the assassins' associates Ciganović and Tankosić, and the illegal border crossing that might not have been feasible without the aid of several Serbian frontier officials. The really crucial part of Wiesner's report, however, consisted of two short and fateful sentences, which he was to rue for the rest of his life. "There is nothing to indicate, or even to give rise to the suspicion," he wired, "that the Serbian government knew about the plot, its preparation, or the procurement of arms. On the contrary, there are indications that this is impossible."

This, then, was the telegram for which the Austrians had been willing to postpone immediate, drastic action. Now that it had arrived, Vienna was worse off than it had been on June 28. Berchtold and the war party still felt that no matter what Wiesner might say, the time had come to move against Serbia—but where was the evidence that would convince anyone but the converted?

It was the triumph of Dimitrijević's planning. Nor would the Austrians learn much more when the trial of the assassins was held in October. The defendants, on that occasion, handled themselves with the same courage, intelligence, and determination they had shown all along.

Neither Princip nor Čabrinović were sentenced to death. Both were under twenty and, under Austrian law, exempt from the death penalty. Some of their helpers were less lucky, and Princip and Čabrinović themselves were to die in prison of tuberculosis a cruelly short time before the end of the war. Few members of the conspiracy survived them for long. Dimitrijević, in fact, preceded them in death. In 1917, he was executed by his own government, apparently for engaging in one plot too many. As this is being written, only two of the assassins are still known to be alive, local boys who were with Princip on the streets of Sarajevo on June 28. One, when last heard from, was chairman of the department of history at the University of Belgrade, the other the curator of the Sarajevo museum he helped to prevent Franz Ferdinand from visiting that Sunday.

• *No More Cause for War? Austrian Ultimatum and Serbian Reply (July 23–25)* Evidence or not, Berchtold, in mid July, was resolved on humiliating Serbia. An unrestrained Serbia, he felt, posed a vital threat to the Habsburg monarchy, no matter who had sent Princip to Sarajevo. If there was no proof linking Pašić's government to the assassination, that was a pity, but Sarajevo, after all, was merely one provocation among many. He would, in one last gamble to save the monarchy, confront Serbia with a number of all but unacceptable demands; and when these had predictably been refused, he would set the army in motion against Belgrade.

What would Serbia's allies do? The answer arrived even before Berchtold's ministry was finished drafting its ultimatum to Serbia. Supposedly, the ultimatum was being prepared in the strictest secrecy, and the Austrians certainly took great pains not to frighten their German ally with any advance information about its contents. But rumors about what was going on in Vienna were spreading. On July 18, Serge Sazonov, Russia's foreign minister, thought it necessary to take the Austrian ambassador aside and tell him that "Russia would not be indifferent to any effort to humiliate Serbia. Russia would not permit Austria to use menacing language or military measures against Serbia. In short: *'La politique de la Russie est pacifique mais pas passive.'*"

But would Russia really dare to move? Austria had Germany's blank check; how could Russia cope with an Austro-German coalition? The answer came in terms as clear as those of Sazonov's warning. On July 20, Raymond Poincaré, President of the French Republic, arrived in St. Petersburg for a state visit. The next day, during a reception of the diplomatic corps, he asked the Austrian ambassador if he had any news of the Serbian affair, and on receiving an evasive answer, said: "With a little good will, this Serbian business is easy to settle. But it can just as easily become acute. Serbia has some very warm friends in the Russian people. And Russia has an ally, France."

Work on the Austrian ultimatum continued as though neither Sazonov nor Poincaré had spoken. On July 23, it was finished. At 6 P.M. it was presented in Belgrade. It was a brutal document whose directness had few precedents in diplomatic history.

The Belgrade government, read the ultimatum, was to put an immediate stop to all Serbian sponsored subversive activities on the territory of the Austro-Hungarian monarchy, as well as to all anti-Austrian propaganda in Serbia itself. As a specific instance, the *Narodna Odbrana,* or *National Defense,* a secret organization pursuing Greater Serbian aims, was to be disbanded. Judicial proceedings, the ultimatum went on, were to be instituted against any person in Serbia who had been an accessory to the Sarajevo crime, with "agencies delegated by the Imperial and Royal [Austrian] Government" taking part in any investigation that might, in this connection, be undertaken in Serbia. Tankosić and Ciganović (the two Serbian helpers mentioned by the assassins) were to be arrested "forthwith." The Serbian government was to cooperate in putting an end to the illegal traffic in arms across the border, and the Serbian officials who had aided Princip in crossing the border were to be punished.

The Serbian government had precisely forty-eight hours in which to decide whether to accept or reject these demands: "The Austria-Hungarian Government expects a reply of the Royal Government by 6 P.M., Saturday July 25 at the latest."

Good as Austria-Hungary's basic case against Serbia was, it had been all but destroyed by the ultimatum's text and timing. For all the ultimatum's harsh language, there was no solid evidence linking the Serbian government with the assassination. Tankosić and Ciganović were minor figures. Mention of the *Narodna Odbrana* was next to meaningless, since that organization, while once indeed as menacing as the Black Hand, had meanwhile turned respectable and by 1914 bore roughly the same relation to Colonel Dimitrijević's group that Kropotkin's anarchism bore to Bakunin's. Fine points, perhaps, that might have gone unnoticed, had not so much time been allowed to pass since June 28. What people saw at the end of July 1914 was not an archduke gasping "Stay alive for our children's sake" to a wife who was bleeding to death as fast as he was, but a large nation bullying a small one.

It was hardly strange, then, that when the powers learned of the ultimatum to Serbia on the morning of July 24, they did not rush to Austria's side. The Russians, in fact, quickly did the opposite: in a meeting held that afternoon, the council of ministers gave its approval—which the Tsar endorsed a day later—to a proposal submitted by Sazonov stating that if such a move were to appear useful, several Russian army corps be mobilized against Austria. The British were more pacific. Sir Edward Grey proposed a conference between the four major nations not directly involved—Germany, Italy, France, and Great Britain—to mediate the conflict. Other

capitals withheld action for the time being. All now realized that Europe was facing a major crisis, but before
making any irrevocable decisions, they would await the
Serbian reply.

On July 25, at 5:58 P.M.—two minutes before Vienna's
ultimatum was about to expire—the Austrian envoy in
Belgrade received that answer. In tone and content, it
was remarkably conciliatory.

The Serbian government, the note promised, would, as
soon as parliament met, introduce a press law providing
the most severe penalties for any "incitement to hatred
and contempt of the Austro-Hungarian Monarchy." It
would dissolve the *Narodna Odbrana* even though, as the
Serbians dryly noted, the Austrians had provided them
with no proof of any illegal action on the part of that
organization. It would "severely punish" the frontier officials who had allowed the Sarajevo assassins to cross into
Austria. It would "reinforce and extend the measures
which have been taken for preventing the illicit traffic
in arms and explosives across the frontier."

In fact, the Serbian note agreed to just about all of the
demands of the Austrian ultimatum. There were only
two exceptions. One concerned the arrest of Ciganović,
the other the investigation into the origins of the assassination. Tankosić, said the note, had been taken into custody, but Ciganović, unfortunately, had managed to evade
arrest. As for any participation of Austro-Hungarian
agencies in investigating the crime on Serbian soil, the
government regretted that it was unable to "accede to such
an arrangement, as it would be a violation of the Con-
stitution and of criminal procedure."

Compliance on either point might, of course, have
meant disaster to the Serbians. Belgrade was neither in
a position to permit an investigation that might uncover
a trail leading to the chief of Serbian army intelligence,
nor could it afford to have the Austrian police interrogate
Ciganović. Ciganović, who held an Austrian passport and

whose extradition, unlike Tankosić's, could therefore not very well be denied, had accordingly been warned some weeks before to vanish from sight; and while the precise circumstances of his disappearance may never become public knowledge, there is some room for impugning the zeal with which the Belgrade police set about the task of finding him.

At the time, both seemed minor points. The mood, rather, was one of relief at Serbia's concessions, apparent and real. William II expressed the feelings of many when he wrote after reading the note: "A brilliant performance for a time limit of only 48 hours! A great moral success for Vienna, but with it, all reason for war is gone. . . ."

He had misread Austria's intentions even more badly than Serbia's reply. For the Austrians fully intended to take offense, no matter what Pašić might say to them. Within minutes of being handed the Serbian note, and after no more than a glance at its contents, the Austrian envoy told Pašić that he considered the document unsatisfactory and that he, therefore, had "the honor to inform Your Excellency . . . . that from the moment this letter reaches Your Excellency the rupture in the diplomatic relations between Serbia and Austria-Hungary will have the nature of a *fait accompli*." At 6:30, 32 minutes after the receipt of the note, the envoy and his staff were at the Belgrade terminal, catching the train home. Three-and-a-half hours later, the Austrian chief of staff received Imperial orders to mobilize the armed forces of Austria-Hungary against Serbia.

• *Peace or War? The Small War Begins* (*July 25–28*)
Europe began to prepare for the worst, while still hoping for the best. Earlier on July 25, the Tsar had given his approval to Russia's partial mobilization. (The extent to which this decision strengthened Pašić in his resolve to resist full compliance with the Austrian demands has remained subject to much scholarly debate.) Later that

day, the French, very discreetly, lest they be accused of aggressive intentions, took some precautionary military measures. A day later, the admiralty in London ordered the British fleet, which had been assembled in review and was ready to disperse, to remain at its stations. But at the same time, the statesmen were trying for peace, or at least for a localization of the conflict.

The Germans concentrated on ways of restricting the conflict, if war should come, to the original parties to the dispute, Austria and Serbia. The Tsar had the sudden inspiration of submitting the whole matter to the International Tribunal of Justice at the Hague. The more practical British—the Tsar's suggestion, in fact, never passed beyond Sazonov's desk—reverted, in a more precise form now, to their earlier idea of a four power conference: let the ambassadors of France, Germany, and Italy in London, said Sir Edward Grey on July 26, meet with him and search for ways to resolve the conflict. The Italians promptly accepted the proposal. So did the French, although with a notable lack of enthusiasm. The Germans alone, on July 27, refused. It was their greatest blunder since the day of the blank check; they were still under the illusion that they could localize the conflict.

It did not take them long to recognize their error. Later that same day, after a hard look at the diplomatic dispatches that had been pouring in, the Germans faced the bitter truth that if Austria and Serbia were to fight, so would Russia, France, and quite possibly Great Britain. Now the Germans radically altered their course. Might it not be wise, they urgently asked Vienna on the evening of July 27, to accept the Serbian reply as a basis for negotiation?

It was too late. Come what may, the Austrian government was resolved to end what it considered the Serbian threat to the empire's survival. On Tuesday, July 28, without any further consultation with Berlin, the Habsburg monarchy declared war on the kingdom of Serbia.

• *"Mobilization Means War": The Intervention of Russia* (*July 25–29*) The small war had begun. Frantically, Europe's leaders tried to prevent a larger one.

The historian, in recounting their efforts, is aware of a basic problem of historiography, that any comprehensible narrative of what took place in the ministries and palaces of Europe during the days following July 28 must of necessity contain some element of falsehood. For what in print is likely to look neat and logical, in truth, more often than not, was chaotic or at best improvised. Decisions were made with no time for proper reflection, messages crossed each other, and some of the most fateful errors were committed from motives no more profound or sinister than lack of information or sleep. It is with this in mind that we should view the events that occurred between the last days of July and the opening days of August 1914.

One of the most sensible proposals for saving the general peace now came from the Kaiser. In normal times, William II could be insufferable, a crowned buffoon without peer; in this moment of crisis, he was acting with as clear a head as anyone. Let the Austrians, he proposed on July 28, halt their armies when they reached Belgrade, and suspend the war. With Serbia's capital as a "pledge," the Austrians could be sure of obtaining some genuine satisfaction from Pašić's government. Meanwhile, there would be a breathing spell, and the powers would be able to gather for sensible peace talks.

Grey rather found himself in sympathy with the suggestion, but Bethmann at first failed to urge it on the Austrians with anything like real vigor. Berchtold remained silent, nor did he respond when Bethmann, on July 29, finally grew more insistent. The time was past when anyone could tell the Austrians just what they might or might not do about the Serbian issue, even if, as now seemed more apparent by the hour, this meant incurring the gravest risk of Russian intervention.

To prevent this sort of extension of the war, the Kaiser, on July 29, sent a telegram to his cousin, the Tsar. Would "Nicky," said "Willy" (salutation and signature are those of the text) realize that he, his Berlin friend and relative, was exerting his "utmost influence to induce the Austrians to arrive at a satisfactory solution with you. I confidently hope that you will help me in my efforts." Nicholas II, it so happened, had been sending a very similar appeal to the Kaiser at just about the same moment, begging him, "in the name of our old friendship," to do what he could "to stop your allies from going too far and to avoid a calamity such as a European war." William II quickly replied that he would, but that one obstacle lay in Russia's apparent military preparations. Berlin was hearing rumors about a Russian mobilization against Austria; if true, the Kaiser warned, this might end all hopes for peace.

It was a point on which the Tsar was willing to accommodate his cousin. But in so indicating, he made a fatal admission. "The military measures which have now come into force," he wired back during the night of July 29 to 30, were no sudden anti-Austrian gesture, but had been "decided on five days ago for reasons of defense on account of Austria's preparations."

The Kaiser was furious. "My work," he said, "is at an end." Here he had been trying to mediate, and what had the Russians done but use his efforts as a cover for obtaining a five days' start in military preparations. Worse was to come. To understand it, it is necessary to go back a few days and deal with the matter of Russia's mobilization in a certain amount of detail.

On July 24, a prominent German businessman and friend of the Kaiser, Albert Ballin, in London for a brief visit, was having dinner with two British acquaintances of his. They were the First Lord of the Admiralty, Winston Churchill, and Churchill's colleague in the war department, Lord Haldane. "I remember," Ballin said to them, "old Bismarck telling the year before he died that one day the great European war would come out of some damned foolish thing in the Balkans." The forecast seemed about to come true. Everything, said Ballin, depended on the Tsar now: What would Nicholas do if Austria were to chastise Serbia? "If Russia marches against Austria, we must march; and if we march, France must march, and what would England do?"

What the Tsar would do was suggest to the Serbians, in the aftermath of Berchtold's ultimatum, that while they should give no gratuitous offense to the Austrians, they might also rest assured that Russia would not remain indifferent to their fate. The Russians calculated that they could not afford a repetition of the Annexation Crisis, which had left the Serbians with the feeling of having been deserted by their Slavic protector. It was—or so it seemed to the men who made policy in St. Petersburg —a choice between taking the risk of war or accepting a major blow to Imperial Russia's prestige and power in the Balkans.

What the Tsar also would do, as we have seen, was to give his advance approval, on July 25, to Russia's partial mobilization against Austria in case of need. To this he added, on that same day, his agreement to issuing the necessary secret orders for a "period preparatory to war." Leaves were to be cancelled, reservists called, Russia's harbors closed—in short, the country would begin to prepare for mobilization. These were some of the measures that had so upset the Kaiser, yet they had seemed essential to Russia's military. War was a possibility, and Russia a vast country. Moving the Russian armed forces to their battle stations would take a very long time, and the nature of modern war was such that the power capable of striking the first blow would have an intolerable advantage. To recall Bret Harte's advice:

> Blest is the man whose cause is just;
> Thrice blest is he who gets his blow in fust.

Under normal circumstances, the Germans and the Austrians, with their better railroad system and their gen-
erally more efficient military machine, would have just
that advantage. Hence, the need on Russia's part to
begin preparing before they did.

On July 28, Sazonov decided that the time had come
to go beyond the steps of the "period preparatory to war,"
and to cash in the Tsar's three-day-old blank check.
Russia, he informed the powers that day, was beginning
the partial mobilization of her armed forces toward Austria. Several considerations accounted for this decision.
One was the Austrian declaration of war against Serbia,
which had come after several urgent appeals of his to
Berchtold for the opening of Austro-Russian talks had
simply gone unanswered. Another was a French reassur-
ance of support. In this moment of supreme danger, the
French were doing no more to restrain their Russian ally
than the Germans had done to hold back the Austrians.

There were, in the French case, more extenuating circumstances than in that of the Germans. Poincaré, President of the Republic, and Viviani, prime minister and
foreign minister as well, were at sea, returning from their
Russian state visit, and out of regular communication with
Paris and Petersburg. "Not to have exact information
about anything," Poincaré later wrote about the voyage,

not even to have the essential data in hand as to the problem
that was to be resolved, caused M. Viviani not only mental but
physical suffering. He paced the *France's* deck in his agitation,
silent for long periods, then returning at intervals affectionately
to pour his anguish into my ear.

In Paris, Bienvenu-Martin, minister of justice and acting
foreign minister in Viviani's absence, knew little of what
was going on, and did not really understand the true seriousness of the crisis. In Petersburg, Paléologue, the
French ambassador, and a strong advocate of the Franco-
Russian alliance, was pursuing a policy of his own. He
deliberately misinformed Paris about what was taking

place in Russia. He also gave promises of support to the Russians which exceeded his instructions. This fairly complex background, however, did not particularly concern or interest Sazonov. What did concern and interest him was what France's official spokesman at Petersburg told him, and that was clear enough. To quote from the diary entry for July 28 of Baron Schilling, Sazonov's *chef de cabinet*: "On the instructions of his Government, the French Ambassador acquainted the Foreign Minister with the complete readiness of France to fulfill her obligations as an ally in case of necessity."

Yet another reason deserves to be mentioned for Russia's decision to begin mobilization: Sazonov, while no fool, was no Nesselrode or Gorchakov either. He was, in fact, no more of a man to have in charge in time of crisis than was Berchtold in Vienna. He was given to moods, and worse, to gambles and to dubious judgments, and he may well have thought that partial mobilization would prevent general war, since it would frighten the Austrians without threatening the Germans.

Things would not work that way. Partial mobilization, he was to learn apparently within hours of deciding on it, was an illusion. The sad and simple fact was that the Russian general staff had no plan for it.

The partial mobilization that Sazonov had in mind would have placed four Russian military districts facing Austria on a war footing. This would have been a provocation. (The Austrians, after all, had restricted their military moves to Serbia and been careful to take no preparatory measures against Russia.) But given its limited scope, it might have been a tolerable provocation. "Might have been," for what now came to light was that the Russian general staff had failed to make any provisions for a limited mobilization against Austria alone. It had not been able to conceive of a war that would not be fought against both of the Central Powers; hence, all its plans provided for general mobilization, that is for mobilization against Germany as well as against Austria.

Then why had the army, in the council of ministers of July 24 where partial mobilization was first tentatively decided on, not said so? It had not, because the chief of the general staff, General Janushkevich, was relatively new to his post—he had assumed it only five months previously —and was still unfamiliar with his office's mobilization plans. Some of his subordinates, better informed than he, soon told him that partial mobilization was next to impossible. It would have to be improvised (a difficult thing to do with a railroad timetable) and lead to nothing but confusion and disorder. It would have to be general mobilization or nothing.

When Sazonov now presented his decision for partial mobilization, Janushkevich had to tell him the bitter truth. No matter what the foreign minister may have thought privately about the intelligence of generals, it seemed too late for him to draw back. Had he known on July 24 that partial mobilization was a myth, he might have chosen a very different course of diplomatic action. But he had not known, and by July 28, he felt irretrievably committed to a policy of strength. He therefore did nothing to counteract the pressure that the military proceeded to put on the Tsar to agree to general mobilization.

On July 29, they had the agreement they wanted. That morning, the Tsar signed the order for general mobilization. Fortunately, it did not go out immediately. Under the rules, the ministers of war, the navy, and the interior were required to countersign it. Prenuclear societies, too, took their precautions, although they could be more leisurely about it, and it was not until evening that the three men had been located. All signed reluctantly. The minister of war knew full well how sadly prepared his army was. His colleague in the navy department realized that his fleet was no match for Germany's. The minister of the interior sensed that war for Russia might be the prelude to revolution. But, making the sign of the cross, he, as the others had done, signed.

What they also knew was that they had, in effect, been

putting their signatures to a declaration of war. No international law specifically stated that mobilization automatically equaled war. It did not have to; the implications were clear.

In 1892, after signing the Military Convention that had just been concluded between his country and Russia, the French delegate, General Boisdeffre (he was, at that time, the deputy chief of the French general staff) had had this to say to the Tsar: "Mobilization is a declaration of war. To mobilize is to oblige's one's neighbor to do the same. Mobilization causes the carrying out of strategic transport and concentration. Otherwise, to allow a million men to mobilize on one's frontiers without at once doing the same oneself is to forfeit all possibility of following suit, is to put oneself in the position of an individual with a pistol in his pocket who allows his neighbor to point a weapon at his head without reaching for his own." To which Nicholas' predecessor, Alexander III, had replied: "That is how I too understand it."

Yet there was still time to put down the weapon. At this point, just about everyone, it seemed, was warning everyone else in Europe to do so. Lord Grey, that Wednesday, July 29, was telling the German ambassador in London that if Germany and France were to be drawn into the Austro-Serbian conflict, England might be unable to stand aside. The Russians, with their military measures, were putting the Austrians on notice. The Germans, by means of the Kaiser's latest "Dear Nicky" telegram, were telling the Russians that their military preparations were jeopardizing the peace. What was more, one person was actually listening. On the evening of July 29, a moment before the orders he had signed that morning were about to go out, the Tsar instructed his generals to cancel general mobilization, and to replace it—whether this be practical or not—with partial mobilization again.

• *Finding, Suicide; Motive, Fear of Death—A Time of Ultimatums (July 30–31)*   That was on Wednesday. On

Thursday, July 30, the Tsar had changed his mind once more. Both his generals and his foreign minister had given him no peace. What the hour demanded, they insisted, was general mobilization, not partial measures. "Think of the responsibility you are asking me to take!" said Nicholas II. "Think of the thousands and thousands of men who will be sent to their death!" He was thinking of them, said Sazonov, but diplomacy's work was done; war was coming. What mattered now was that Russia be prepared.

Late that afternoon, the Tsar surrendered. Sazonov rushed to another room to telephone the chief of staff with the news. "Now," he ended their conversation, "you can smash your telephone. Give your orders, General— and then disappear for the rest of the day."

General mobilization was on again, and no telephone, smashed or whole, would ring to announce any orders to undo it. Most writers have been liberal with their criticism of Nicholas II for his behavior in this time of crisis. But only an extraordinarily strong man could ultimately have resisted the massed opinions of both diplomatic and military experts, and only a very callous man would not have hesitated and hesitated again before giving orders as fateful as these.

The Germans, when they heard the news, were close to panic. Earlier that day, July 30, when he had learned of Russia's partial mobilization, the Kaiser's first anguished comment had been, "That means I have got to mobilize as well." The situation now was infinitely worse. The Russians were moving against them, the Germans, not just against the Austrians. And what would France do but support her Eastern ally? Here it was, the old nightmare of a two-front war, and it was real.

There was only one possibility, the Germans had long thought, of winning such a war. It lay in offsetting the overwhelming advantage in men and material that France and Russia held with speed. If they, the Germans, were to move quickly against the French and to defeat them in a matter of at most six weeks, they might then be able to rush their troops to the east just before the Russians had fully brought their forces into position. To allow the Russians to proceed with their general mobilization and thereby let Germany's only chance of victory slip away seemed intolerable. Or so the military experts in Berlin argued, and as in St. Petersburg, it was they who had the last word.

In the afternoon of Friday, July 31, two ultimatums went out from Berlin, one to Russia, the other to France. Would the Russians, stated the dispatch to St. Petersburg, suspend mobilization within twelve hours or face German mobilization and, by implication, war. Would the French, stated the dispatch to Paris, within eighteen hours give a promise of neutrality in the event of a Russo-German war. Should the French reply be affirmative—an unexpected contingency, since the ultimatum was no more meant to be accepted than Austria's ultimatum to Serbia had been —would they hand Germany the fortresses of Toul and Verdun in token of their good faith. Meanwhile, the Germans were preparing for the all too probable next step by proclaiming, that Friday, a "Threatening Danger of War," which meant that they were taking preliminary military measures just short of mobilization.

". . . And what would England do?" Both Haldane and Churchill had evaded a direct response to Ballin's question, but the answer, though still not final, was becoming fairly plain: Britain, too, was preparing to intervene. On July 31, Lord Grey asked both Germany and France for assurances that they would respect the neutrality of Belgium. The French quickly replied in the affirmative; the Germans were silent. The same day, Sir Eyre Crowe sent a long memorandum to Lord Grey. If, as seemed more likely than not, France and Germany should go to war, then Britain too should fight. "The theory," wrote Crowe,

that England cannot engage in a big war means her abdication
as an independent State. . . . The argument that there is no
written bond binding us to France is strictly correct. There is
no contractual obligation. But the *Entente* has been made,
strengthened, put to the test and celebrated in a manner justi-
fying the belief that a moral bond was being forged. The
whole policy of the *Entente* can have no meaning if it does not
signify that in a just quarrel England would stand by her
friends. This honourable expectation has been raised. We
cannot repudiate it without exposing our good name to grave
criticism.

Almost imperceptibly, everyone's gaze shifted to Germany. The original causes of the crisis no longer seemed
very important. On that same July 31, some eighteen
hours after Russia's mobilization. Austria-Hungary ordered general mobilization. Hardly anyone paid any attention. To Russia and the *Entente* alike, Germany was
becoming the main enemy. The Germans were paying
the price for the distrust and friction that, through design or clumsiness, had been allowed to accumulate over
the past two decades.

• *War* (*August 1–4*)   The events following Russia's mobilization and Germany's resort to ultimatums have something anti-climactic about them. The suicide pacts had
been made; what was happening now, or so it seems in
retrospect, was that the weapons were being raised, and
raised with such resolution and speed that there was no
chance for second thoughts.

On Saturday afternoon, August 1, the French, after re-
jecting the German ultimatum, ordered general mobilization. A quarter of an hour later, the Germans followed
suit; there had been no reply from St. Petersburg to their
ultimatum of the previous day. At about six o'clock that
evening, the German ambassador, Count Pourtalès, called
on Sazonov. Was there truly no hope of a favorable Russian reply to the German demand that mobilization cease?

There was not, said Sazonov. "In that case," said Pourtalès, "I am instructed to hand you this note." He then
gave Sazonov the German declaration of war on Russia,
went to the window, and broke into tears.

It was up to the generals now. Their time to weep
would come too; at the moment, the generals, whether
Russian, Austrian or German, wanted but one thing: to
move! The day before Pourtalès's final visit, a significant
scene had taken place in Vienna. In the midst of Bethmann's appeals to Berchtold to continue negotiating, a
telegram had arrived from Count Moltke, chief of the
German general staff, for his Austrian counterpart in
Vienna, Count Conrad. Stand firm, said the telegram.
Do not negotiate; "mobilize immediately against Russia."
When Conrad showed the message to Berchtold, the foreign minister was taken aback. "Who is in charge?" he
said. "Moltke or Bethmann?"

Moltke, of course. Ever since Russia's final decision to
mobilize, the German generals had been impatient to
begin military operations. They saw no other chance of
victory except to strike first. They wished to defeat
France rapidly and decisively while holding the defensive
in the East and only then to shift their forces to attack
the Russians. The question of course was how the Germans could manage to win such a victory over a France
whose army was among Europe's best and whose border
was heavily fortified. A plan, completed by the general
staff under its then chief, General von Schlieffen, in 1905
provided a theoretical answer. The German army would
circumvent the French fortifications by moving through
Luxembourg and Belgium and take the French forces by
surprise from the North. Would this violate Germany's
treaty obligations toward Belgium? It would, but then,
what was the alternative? Possibly, barely possibly, this
was a justifiable counter-question for a professional soldier
to raise. Possibly also, one should not be too astonished
to find only the briefest references to the probable political

repercussions of the violation of Luxembourg's neutrality ("no important consequences other than protests") in Schlieffen's memorandum of 1905 and none to those of Belgium's. What, however, of Germany's diplomats, who should have known better?

German diplomats, in the post-Bismarck epoch, did not normally care to argue with German generals. If that was what the gentlemen of the general staff held to be essential, said the gentlemen of the Wilhelmstrasse, then that was what German diplomacy must reconcile itself to. To quote the reported comment of Baron von Holstein, one of the senior officials of the German foreign ministry: "If the Chief of the General Staff, and particularly a strategic authority like Schlieffen, thought such a measure to be necessary, then it would be the duty of diplomacy to adjust itself to it and to prepare for it in every possible way." To which we might add "adjust, yes; prepare, no," since at no time between the plan's first draft and 1914 did the foreign ministry lay the least diplomatic groundwork for it.

With the decision to go to war against Russia, the general staff's Western war games became dead earnest. On Saturday, August 1, German troops invaded Luxembourg. On Sunday, August 2, at 7 P.M., the German envoy in Brussels presented an ultimatum to the Belgian foreign minister. (It was drafted mainly by Moltke; the foreign ministry had not prepared so much as the necessary diplomatic note in advance.) Germany, stated the note, to anticipate a French attack and "acting under a dictate of self-preservation," must march through Belgium. Should Belgium agree, the Germans would evacuate all Belgian territory upon the termination of the war and make restitution for any damage done. Should Belgium resist, "Germany would be obliged, to her regret, to regard the Kingdom as an enemy." Would the Belgians give an unequivocal answer within twelve hours.

This was worse than either a crime or a blunder. It

was a disaster. The Germans were not only drawing the Belgians into the war against them; they were destroying all hopes of British neutrality. Quite possibly, England would sooner or later have joined Germany's enemies in any event, but owing to Berlin's lack of judgment, we will never know for certain. The violation of Luxembourg's neutrality had not disturbed the British unduly. (Here, for once, Schlieffen had been right.) It was true that Britain was signatory to a treaty guaranteeing the neutrality of Luxembourg, but the country was very small and possessed no coast line facing the channel. Belgium was different. The day before, the British cabinet had still been divided over what course of action to take. Pressures to intervene were coming from many sides: from the French, from the Conservative opposition in parliament, from the professionals in the foreign office. But the most that Grey had been willing to do had been to promise some naval support to the French in case the German fleet should sail into the channel to attack French shipping or the French coast. The ultimatum to Belgium radically altered the situation. Britain, as a signatory to the Treaty of 1839, was one of the guarantors of Belgian neutrality (Prussia, and hence Germany, was another) and in 1914 as in 1839, Britain considered the defense of Belgium's channel ports all but a part of the defense of the realm. On August 2, the British cabinet decided that if the Germans were indeed to violate Belgian neutrality, and if the Belgians were to resist, Britain would intervene.

Within forty-eight hours, there were no "if's" left. On Monday, August 3, the Belgians rejected the German ultimatum and called on the signatories of the treaty of 1839 for aid. That same day, the Germans began the invasion of Belgium and, on the mendacious pretext that the French had attacked German territory, declared war on France. On Tuesday, August 4, the British sent an ultimatum to Berlin. Would the Germans, within five hours, give an assurance that they were ceasing their attack on

Belgium; if not, the British would sever diplomatic relations.

The Germans rejected the ultimatum. The quick defeat of France, they said, was a matter of life and death to them. One is struck by the ingenuousness of the German response. What the Germans were doing, in effect, was asking the British to understand the requirements of the Schlieffen Plan, and then acting aggrieved when the British did not. The step that Britain was contemplating, said Bethmann, as the British ambassador paid his farewell call on him, "was terrible to a degree, just for a word 'neutrality,' a word which in war time had so often been disregarded—just for a scrap of paper, Great Britain was making war on a kindred nation who desired nothing better than to be friends with her."

Poor honest Bethmann, providing Allied propaganda with some of its most telling quotations. We have become somewhat less solicitous today over the universal observance of international law, but 1914 was another age. That same August 4, Bethmann rose in the Reichstag to say a few more words that, for his country's good, should forever have remained unspoken.

Gentlemen, we are now in a state of self-defense, and necessity knows no law. Our troops have occupied Luxembourg, and perhaps have already entered Belgian territory.

Gentlemen, that is a breach of international law. . . . The wrong—I speak openly—the wrong we thereby commit we will try to make good as soon as our military aims are attained. He who is menaced the way we are, and is fighting for his most precious possessions, can turn his mind only to how he might battle his way out.

At midnight, on August 4, Great Britain declared war on Germany. The Austro-Serbian conflict had escalated before the term had been invented.

Before it was over, the war would have expanded into a truly global conflict. The Central Powers were to gain only two more allies: Turkey, which entered the war in

November 1914, and Bulgaria, which came in the next year. The Triple *Entente,* on the other hand, managed to draw in half the world on its side. Within the next three years, to mention only the major belligerents, Italy (which found new Allied promises more persuasive than old treaty commitments), Portugal, Rumania, Japan, the United States, and China were to join the Allied side.

The generals were in charge, and in August of 1914, a vast majority of people were deliriously happy that this should be so. The declarations of war seemed to have purified the air. In the various capitals of Europe, the crowds gathered—patriotic, fervent, elemental; athirst for victory and ready for sacrifice. "Whoever failed to see Paris this morning and yesterday," wrote Charles Péguy on August 3, "has seen nothing."[1] He would not try to describe his journey to the front, wrote a French officer that same week; "sunshine cannot be reproduced adequately on a painting."[2]

A few days earlier, after Berchtold had made his irrevocable decision on Serbia, the Bohemian writer Johannes Urzidil was walking through the streets of Prague. Coming to a tobacco shop, he noticed a group of people congregating around a telegram posted in the window:

"War Declared"
No one spoke. Then I suddenly heard three lone words: *"Gott sei Dank"*—"Thank God."
The speaker was an Austrian first lieutenant. He did not try to give any reasons why one should especially thank God for this declaration of war. What will have become of him?. . .
All I know is that the words "Thank God" soon changed into the much more fitting ones: "God help us!"[3]

---

[1] Quoted in Paul Marie de la Gorce, *The French Army* (George Braziller, New York, 1963), p. 94.

[2] Quoted in Richard Thoumin, *The First World War* (G. B. Putnam's Sons, New York, 1963), p. 31.

[3] Johannes Urzidil, "In Prag," *Der Monat* (August 1964), p. 41.

5   A Question
of Responsibility

• *"Argument without End"*   How had it happened?
The victors, in 1919, were very certain of the answer—
the Central Powers had willfully begun this most terrible
of wars! The Germans, in Article 231 of the Treaty of
Versailles, were made to admit their war guilt: "The
Allied and Associated Governments affirm and Germany
accepts the responsibility of Germany and her allies for
causing all the loss and damage to which the Allied and
Associated Governments and their nationals have been
subjected as a consequence of the war imposed upon them
by the aggression of Germany and her allies."

Thirty-three years later, a committee of French and
German historians, engaged in an over-all effort at re-
moving some of the grosser errors of fact and judgment
from both nation's textbooks, agreed on the following,
rather different, statement: "The documents do not permit attributing, to any government or nation, a premeditated desire for European war in 1914. Distrust was
at its highest, and leading groups were dominated by the
thought that war was inevitable; everyone thought that
the other side was contemplating aggression. . . ."

Between these two statements, tons of documents, books,
and articles bearing on the cause of the First World War
made their appearance. Their often very different presen-
tations of what ought essentially to be the same facts are

enough to shake anyone's faith in the feasibility of historical objectivity. And the argument is not over yet. Nor should it be. We all have good reason for wanting to discover how, particularly if no one really wished it, a world war of such proportions could occur. We also possess an advantage not of our own making: we should be far enough removed from the time, the place, and the passions of these events to reach some fair and sober judgments. What follows, then, is an attempt to do just that, although throughout, it will be well to bear in mind that splendid phrase of the great Dutch historian, Pieter Geyl, about "that argument without end which to us of the West is the study of history." Or, in the words of one of Theodor Fontane's Prussian squires: "Unassailable truths don't exist, or if they do, they are dull."

• *National Responsibility:* AUSTRIA AND SERBIA Let us begin by considering what, in descending order, each nation's share of the responsibility was. This is a consciously old-fashioned approach. The tendency, once the hatreds of the war had faded, was to emphasize less directly national causes of the war. But matters such as the alliance system, imperialism, national sovereignty, or the powers of the press were realities with which every statesman had to contend; they were a part of the atmosphere that affected all of Europe. How then did each nation manage its affairs in the real world in which it had to live and not in an ideal one of no entangling alliances, of colonial satiety, of the rule of world law, or of a press that promoted nothing but knowledge and love?

The nation that managed its affairs least well in 1914 was Austria-Hungary. We have stood stooped over too long now, searching for the underlying causes of the war. We have become so involved with subtleties that the obvious has sometimes escaped us—we have not seen the forest for the roots. The obvious fact is that it was the Austrian ultimatum of July 23 that not only invited war with Serbia but laid the basis for general war as well. What an appalling document it was—tardy, incompetent, deceptive, designed to be rejected. Austria was setting the course, and neither friend nor foe had been allowed an honest look at its direction.

It is entirely possible, of course, to present a case for the defense. Sarajevo was no pretense; the Habsburg monarchy had some perfectly legitimate interests to defend— Serbia was a good deal closer to Austria than Southeast Asia is to the United States. Surely, self-preservation is as sensible and honorable a motive as any, and the state one wished to maintain had a great deal to be said in its favor. "My whole libido," wrote Dr. Freud the day after Serbia's reply had been received, "goes out to Austria-Hungary."

But to understand all is *not* to forgive all. It was true enough that no government or nation had "a premeditated desire for European war in 1914." But Austria, in 1914, had very much of a premeditated desire for a small Balkan war. Did it want that war to spread? No, but the truth was that the reckless and inadequate people who were deciding policy in Vienna did not really care. This was Austria's war; perhaps only the fact that the countrymen of Johann Strauss and Sigmund Freud ordinarily made such poor villains (there would be some fairly obvious exceptions such as Adolf Hitler) allowed that simple fact to be forgotten so thoroughly.

Austria's war, and Serbia's. Colonel Dimitrijević, too, had not much cared what the repercussions of Franz Ferdinand's murder might be. Had he known that his deed would mean war, said one of the assassins during his trial, he would have preferred his own death to that of his victim. It is not likely that he was speaking for Dimitrijević. But to what extent did the action of Serbia's chief of army intelligence incriminate his government? The murder, after all, had been planned by the Black Hand during the colonel's off-duty hours and not by Pašić or any of his ministers.

Dimitrijević's action did incriminate the Serbian government, for reasons both long-range and immediate. The government had for too many years been tolerating or even encouraging a movement for a Greater Serbia, whose aims were bound to be offensive to Austria-Hungary, and whose methods were bound to be offensive to anyone. Very specifically speaking, the government in 1914 had taken no effective action to prevent the assassination of Franz Ferdinand, of which it very probably had some fore-knowledge, nor had it managed to end the influence of the Black Hand, of which it assuredly had knowledge.

Again, there was nothing ignoble about either Pašić's or Dimitrijević's aims. The concept of a Greater South Slav State was fully as defensible as was Austria-Hungary's right to survival. Tragedy, in the Hegelian definition, consists not of the conflict of right with wrong but of right with right. But the Serbians set about achieving their purposes with a truly frightening disregard of the consequences. Here, then, was Serbia's vast share in the responsibility for the First World War, one that was matched only by Austria's: Belgrade surely knew that it was set on collision course, yet it would not alter direction. There is, in the British files, a report from the ambassador to Vienna, Sir Fairfax Cartwright, written in January 1913 in connection with another, milder crisis brought about by Pan-Serb agitation, which sums up the entire matter better than any later historian can:

Serbia will some day set Europe by the ears, and bring about a universal war on the Continent. I cannot tell you how exasperated people are getting here at the continual worry which that little country causes to Austira under encouragement from Russia. It will be lucky if Europe succeeds in avoiding war on account of the present crisis. The next time a Serbian crisis arises, I feel sure that Austria-Hungary will refuse to admit of any Russian interference in the dispute and that she will proceed to settle her difference with her little neighbor coûte que coûte.

• RUSSIA AND GERMANY   Russian encouragement and Russian interference—one wonders how different Serbia's course of action might have been in 1914 without these. In the sixty years that preceded Sarajevo, Russia had been involved directly in two wars—the Crimean War and the War of 1877–1878—indirectly in two more—the Balkan Wars of 1912 and 1913—and, directly or indirectly, in crises too numerous to list, all with the intent of weakening the empire of the Sultan to the benefit of that of the Tsar. It was a policy that acted as an irritant to Austro-Russian relations; threats to one's survival tend to annoy. Yet the Russians persisted. It was Russia rather than Austria that was the expansionist power in Southeastern Europe. The Annexation Crisis was the exception, not the rule. Under ordinary circumstances, Austria had considerably more to fear from Russia's Balkan ambitions than Russia had from Austria's, even if we add the reservation that customarily, Russian official policy was more restrained and rational than some of the truly extravagant Pan-Slav spokesmen would have liked. Customarily, for in July 1914, as it had on some previous occasions, the borderline between Pan-Slavism and government policy once more became blurred. If Serbia chose to resist Austria's demands, then Russia would support its Slavic brethren. The story of Germany's "blank check" to Austria is well known, but the Russians were doing no better at counseling caution to Belgrade.

Perhaps they had no real choice. Caution would have equalled surrender, and 1908 was too recent a memory. This time, the alternative to active military aid might indeed have been a grave diminution of Russian influence not only in Serbia but throughout the Balkans. Certainly the Austrians had had no reason to assume that Russia would merely look on, let alone look the other way, while they were shooting their way into Belgrade.

The Russian response, however, consisted of more than a move to halt the Austrians. Had Russia mobilized her

forces against Austria only, a negotiated peace, taking both
Russia's and Austria's legitimate interests into account,
might still have been possible. The Russians did not do
this. Instead, and here we come to Russia's quite stagger-
ing responsibility for World War I, they decided to
marshal their forces against Germany as well as against
Austria. Their reasons· for general mobilization were
technical rather than political; honest error and the absence of flexible military planning rather than premeditated design accounted for the Tsar's final decision on
July 30. But no amount of explaining can change two
facts. One was that Russia, in 1914, was the first power to
mobilize. The other was that the Tsar and his advisers,
by their behavior on July 29 and 30, showed that they
were perfectly well aware of what mobilization meant.

What, though, of Germany's guilt? Was the Versailles
indictment really that absurd? Surely, it could not have
been due entirely to the machinations of Allied propaganda that Germany was seen as the chief culprit in 1914
and not Russia, Austria, or Serbia, or that so many subsequent accounts (this one included) written in a more
temperate climate of opinion, would place Germany so
close to the center of the narrative.

German responsibility for 1914 goes back at least to
the 1890s, to the whole conduct of German diplomacy
after Bismarck. The master's touch was shown by moderation, the touch of his successors by what Bismarck had
accused post-Cavour Italy of: a large appetite and poor
teeth. And to what did Germany's appetite really run
after 1890? To "world power," to rivalry with Britain,
to a German Central Africa, to security against France?
None of these policies had been thought through. Activity there was aplenty; what was lacking was direction.

By 1914, as a result of the behavior of the Kaiser and of
too many of the men close to him, a new specter had come
to haunt Europe: the specter of *furor teutonicus*. German
behavior in the final crisis certainly did little to banish it.

The list of German blunders is an all too familiar one: the blank check to Austria; the failure, once it had become plain that an Austro-Serbian war was likely to become European in scope, to search for a compromise with every last ounce of energy; the final triumph of the military over the political rationale with the invasion of Belgium and France.

The list is so familiar that one is tempted to point out that there is another side to it. One is especially tempted to do so in the light of the discussion initiated by the Hamburg historian Fritz Fischer. Fischer has maintained, in one of the most stimulating of recent reinterpretations of modern diplomatic history, that Germany's leadership had a will to war in 1914, and it was Germany, with its "bid for world power" and its readiness to engage in conflict with Russia and France, that bore a crucial part of the responsibility for the castastrophe.

Now it is disarming, and probably very healthy beside, to have a historian take this critical a look at his own nation's recent history. What is wrong with it, however, and with general allegations of Germany's war guilt as well, is that it involves a certain amount of confusion between Germany's war aims as they ultimately developed and Germany's intentions in July 1914. What is wrong with it, too, is that it depends for its effect on viewing Germany's actions in isolation. Germany indeed wished to be a great power, and why not? The concept of a German Samoa was no more absurd than that of a British Bahamas or a Belgian Congo.

Germany, the distinction may be worth spelling out, wished to be a world power; it did not aim at world domination. To be sure, during the course of the war, some fairly grotesque German war aims emerged, from the annexation of Belgian iron mines to the establishment of a German Central Africa. But two things need to be noted. One is that Allied war aims were hardly more restrained. The Russians, French, and British were equally busy composing memoranda (and in some cases binding treaties) on the dismemberment of Austria, the truncation of Germany, the transfer of the Dardanelles to Russia, the acquisition of vast tracts of the Ottoman Empire by Britain and France. The other is that in August 1914, Germany no more went to war for Belgian iron ore than Russia did for the Straits or Britain for Palestine. That appetite grew with the eating. Motives are seldom simple, of course, and one might say that expansionist thoughts were in the back of some statesmen's minds that summer, but that was exactly where they were, not in front. In the mountains of documents on the origin of World War I, we search in vain for any that will show us that the statesmen of Germany or of any other nation (with the possible exception of Serbia) went to war in 1914 for the sake of their later war aims.

None of this absolves the Germans from their share in the responsibility. But it is a share only, to be divided with at least five other powers. Germany's responsibility, to reiterate the point, lies in the general foolishness with which the nation behaved in the quarter century before Sarajevo and, more immediately, in the panicky and pernicious decisions that Berlin made during the July crisis. These things were bad enough; there is no need to add imaginary guilt to real guilt.

• BRITAIN AND FRANCE Was it really five powers with which the Germans shared the responsibility? That Germany could point to Russia's mobilization, that Russia in turn to Austria's threat against Serbia, and Austria to Serbia's initial provocation should be obvious, but were not Britain and France innocent bystanders? Not quite.

England's responsibility, stronger even than that of France, lay not in the allegedly insufficient warning the British gave the Germans of their intent to fight, the warning that was so widely discussed in the years immediately after 1914. Surely, any responsible German statesman should have known that it was a matter of vital interest to Great Britain whether France survived as a power and who would control the channel ports of Belgium and France. The implications of the *Entent Cordiale,* and the very plain provisions of the Treaty of 1839, were quite sufficient warning here.

What was involved in the case of Britain was something more long-range. There had taken place, in the half century or so before the war, a tremendous expansion of British power, accompanied by a pronounced lack of sympathy for any similar ambitions on the part of other nations. If any nation was compensation-conscious, it was Great Britain; if the Austrians wished to occupy Bosnia, for instance, then the British must have Cyprus. Even without this particular diplomatic gambit, the British, between the eighteen-seventies and the turn of the century, were adding, adding, adding to their Empire: Burma, Egypt, Uganda, Somaliland, Kenya, Zanzibar, Rhodesia, the Boer Republic, all were flying the Union Jack. If any nation had truly made a bid for world power, it was Great Britain. In fact, it had more than bid for it. It had achieved it. The Germans were merely talking about building a railway to Baghdad. The Queen of England *was* Empress of India. If any nation had upset the world's balance of power, it was Great Britain.

The usually more modest appetites of others, however, were a different matter. That the French in Morocco or the Germans in South West Africa were doing quite as well as colonizers as were the British in Uganda was something that seemed all but impossible to perceive through the London fog. British territorial acquisitions were a part of the progress of mankind; those of others were a menace to world peace and civilization. Russia's desire for access to the Mediterranean was a provocation; Britannia Rule the Waves reflected a noble and natural sentiment.

After the turn of the century, this attitude was directed

with special force at Germany, although it was seldom made clear just what the Germans were to do with all *their* excess energy. Some of the British documents of the period convey an impression of near-hysteria in the face of a rising Germany, reaching from a British admiral's simple suggestion, cited before, to sink the German fleet without warning, to the more erudite memoranda of some of the senior officials of the foreign office decrying the German menace. Unfortunately, if one nation imagines for long enough that another is a menace—"the natural enemy" of Sir Eyre Crowe's phrase—the likelihood is strong that that other nation will some day have to play the role it has been assigned.

That judgment does not exculpate the Germans, who had been willing to endorse a Balkan war that clearly contained the risk of a war in the West. As far as Great Britain's direct responsibility for the final crisis and the outbreak of hostilities is concerned, it is indisputably less than Germany's. It was units of the German army, not of the British navy, who were sending shells into Belgium. Before the guns had been moved into position, however, it can scarcely be said that the British did much better in restraining the Eastern member of the Triple *Entente* than they would accuse the Germans of doing vis-à-vis Vienna. "Will to war" is too grand and at the same time elusive a term to use with any degree of comfort, but what do we do about the memory of what would happen a quarter of a century later? In 1938, when the British definitely did not wish war, their prime minister would hurry to Germany three times within the space of two weeks and negotiate peace under terms far worse than those of 1914 with a leader infinitely more dangerous than the Kaiser in his most Wagnerian moods. The lamps were not "going out" (Lord Grey's celebrated figure of speech) in 1914. Many people, the author of the phrase included, were helping to put them out.

Last of all, there is the responsibility of France—last

of all, and least of all. Had the ultimate decision been
that of France, the lamps would have remained lit.

It was true that a generation or more after Frankfurt,
the French still had not really reconciled themselves to
the loss of Alsace and Lorraine. Poincaré and his friends
were still pursuing what Boulanger had, except that
they were doing so with greater intelligence, tact, patience,
and skill and, hence, with greater effectiveness. The desire to undo the decision of Frankfurt was as powerful a
motive force in France's system of alliances as any. Germany, to put the matter differently, did not wish for any
territorial change in Europe between 1871 and 1914;
France did. It was equally true that during the July crisis,
France failed to urge restraint on St. Petersburg. One
cannot very well indict the Germans for their blank check
to Austria without noting that the Russians held a similar
piece of paper from France.

Yet when compared with the involvement of other nations, how mild the responsibility of France must appear.
The French might mourn Strasbourg, but they were plot-
ting no war to recover it. Even the most irreconcilable
groups of Frenchmen were organizing no Pan-Gallic move-
ments; there was nothing in France to compare, for ambition and folly, with either the Pan-Slavs or the Pan-Germans. Also, all speculations about France's ultimate objectives have about them a certain irrelevancy. Perhaps
France would, some day, have fought to avenge Sedan,
perhaps France would not. We will never know. The
fact is that the French, in August 1914, did not go to war
for Alsace, but because the Germans, lacking the political
imagination and the diplomatic skill to keep France
neutral, first presented an unacceptable ultimatum and
then began to march on Paris. The British had an element of choice, even after the Schlieffen Plan had gone
into operation (major segments of British opinion certainly thought so); the French did not.

In 1914, the French entered the war because they had

no alternative. The Germans had attacked them. It was
that simple.

• *Other Causes, Other Reasons: Diplomacy to Public Opinion* Were not certain other factors more complex, however? What of the forces which transcended traditional
national responsibility: the alliance system, the role of
economic motives, or the impact of imperialism, nationalism, and the press?

Having dealt with these topics before, what can be said
rather summarily here is that while these factors unques-
tionably affected the atmosphere of 1914, and usually for
the worse, none of them, by themselves, were enough to
cause a war.

The alliance system, with its resulting division of
Europe into two camps, did contribute to transforming
Austria's war into general war. But the alliances were
effect, not cause. They were the traditional and legitimate
instruments of each nation's often equally legitimate and
traditional objectives, and not ends in themselves. Nor
were the alliances nearly so firm and automatic as they
sometimes appear in historical literature. They certainly
were considerably less integrated than the system of alliances, both East and West, that emerged after the Second
World War. Italy, for instance, would remain neutral in
1914 despite its formal treaty obligations to the Central
Powers. The Ottoman Empire, on the other hand, would
join them even in the absence of any such ties. In fact,
one might well advance the proposition that if only the
alliances had been stronger—if only Austria-Hungary had
been absolutely certain that an attack on Belgrade meant
an attack on St. Petersburg, if only there had been no
doubt at all in the Germans' minds that a move against
Brussels was a move against London—everything might
still have ended, if not well, at least short of disaster.

There is even less strength in the economic argument,
so tempting to Marxist historians. That economic rivalry,

particularly between Germany and Great Britain, did not appreciably contribute to international amity was quite apparent; but few were the businessmen who would risk the destruction of their entire national economy for the sake of increasing their share in the export market. Businessmen were altogether capable of seeing the advantages of peace, and of economic cooperation. In the case of the Berlin to Baghdad Railway scheme, for instance, British and French bankers were very much in favor of participating along with their German confreres; it was their governments that persuaded them to abstain. And in 1914, businessmen, particularly in Britain and Germany, were as vociferous as anyone, workers included, in opposing war.

Nor should the influence of imperialism or even of the press be exaggerated. Conflicting colonial ambitions did add to Europe's ill temper, especially where Anglo-German relations were concerned. But then, they were an equal burden on Anglo-Russian and Anglo-French relations; yet in 1914, England, Russia, and France found it perfectly possible to fight on the same side. The press, with its tendency to exacerbate or invent diplomatic crises, with its daily offerings of international disaster (potential, imagined, or real), and with its habitual blurring of the distinction between patriotism and chauvinism, may have more to answer for. But public opinion alone can create no wars. If it could, the French would have gone to war against the British at the time of Fashoda and the Serbians and Russians against the Austrians at the time of the annexation crisis. Even William Randolph Hearst, once we separate fact from legend, was not able to deliver a Spanish-American War quite by himself.

• *The Matter of Militarism* One topic that cannot be dealt with quite so cavalierly is the question of militarism. Militarism is a vague and emotional term, so let it be said that two fairly specific aspects of it will be of concern here: the amount of arms available in 1914, and the more than occasional preponderance of military over political considerations.

The military expenditures of the European powers, as noted before, rose at an unprecedented rate in this period, until, at the beginning of 1914, they stood at 300 percent of what they had been in 1870. While the amount of weapons was thus very clearly measurable, the influence on policy was a more subtle matter. Yet Hegel's observation that at some point quantity will change quality was as true as ever. There were too many deadly weapons about for their owners' good in 1914 Europe. With all these splendid instruments of destruction available, it would have been surprising if there had not been a few people who had no marked aversion to seeing them tested.

Their numbers were small, but Berchtold was too close to them and so was Janushkevich. This brings us to the second and even more critical aspect of the matter, the undue influence of military over political decision making. The Germans and the Russians were the worst, though not the only, sinners here. Instead of serving policy, the preparations undertaken by Russia's and Germany's military authorities—general mobilization and Schlieffen Plan—decided policy and, in the event, disastrously so.

Relatively little blame attaches to the generals. It is their task to prepare for war and victory. Nor were the generals always automatically members of the war party. In January 1914, for instance, when Sazonov had advocated the forcible seizure of the Straits, it was the Russian military experts who had opposed the venture on the grounds of its impracticability. A great deal of blame, on the other hand, attaches to the statesmen. It was they who should have known how stretchable a term "military necessity" was, who should have seen how perilous the plans of their respective general staffs were and have countermanded them.

Why they did not do so is not an entirely easy question to answer. One can say that they were men of limited gifts who lacked the qualities necessary to establish the absolute priority of civilian over military authority, such as toughness, intelligence, or the ability to keep regular office hours. (Berchtold and Sazonov, one suspects, were so much the prisoners of their generals' plans in July 1914 largely because they had previously been too lazy to find out what those plans were.) And one can add that it was in those countries where the military stood at the top of the social hierarchy—attracting talent and bestowing prestige as perhaps no other profession did—that there occurred the worst violation of the rule, essential to sound government and sane diplomacy alike, that the sovereign must be commander-in-chief, not the commander-in-chief sovereign.

But this is not the whole answer. For in Britain and France, too, membership in the general staff tended to be an indication of more than usual intelligence and social acceptability. Nor did the military staff talks held under the shelter of the *Entente Cordiale* invariably follow the instructions of the representatives of people or crown; in the summer of 1914, the majority of the British cabinet would be quite as surprised by the obligations incurred toward France as was the majority of the German government by the modalities of the Schlieffen Plan. Still, there were some rather important differences in degree. Thus the French government, when presented with its counterpart of the Schlieffen Plan, providing for a French invasion of Belgium, told the general staff to discard it and to submit a politically more tenable one. And while the professional soldiers of all nations were perhaps equally fascinated by the technological necessities of modern warfare, it was in Russia and Germany again that technology was allowed its clearest triumph over diplomacy.

World War I, as Herman Kahn has been among the first to point out, was to a large extent a war of railroad timetables: "the general staffs of the four great continental powers had spent decades planning meticulous time-tables. The war plans were literally cast in concrete in the sense that governments built railroads according to the requirements of the war plan."[1] Now the advantages of railroads, demonstrated on a large scale first in the American Civil War and then in the Franco-Prussian War, were considerable. They could be used to deploy large armies quickly, effectively, and cheaply and to transport these armies to fight on territory other than one's own. But the system also was notably rigid. A horse can change direction at the flick of the bridle, not so a train. Once set in motion, how was it to be stopped? Even if stopped, how could it be redirected without creating havoc with the remainder of the schedule? Hence, in the Russo-German impasse over mobilization, very much more was involved than diplomatic precedent or prestige. The means of war were being allowed to bring about a state of war.

The final irony was that as the armies began to move, not one of the carefully calculated timetables would really work. Everyone's plans had been predicated on swift and surprising movement, on quick and decisive victory, on precisely the sort of thing that would not come to pass. What no one had anticipated, to make a long mistake very short, was that the war they were about to fight was World War I.

• *"A Tremendous Lack of Imagination"* That was hardly the only miscalculation. Everyone was so intrigued by what might happen if he did *not* risk war that he failed to perceive the cost of violence. The alternatives to war, in the innocent summer of 1914, thus seemed very much worse than war itself. The Austrians were mortally afraid that if they did not march, they might forfeit the final

---

[1] Herman Kahn, *On Thermonuclear War* (Princeton University Press, 1961), p. 359.

opportunity to save their empire. The Russians felt
that they could not possibly leave their Serbian allies to
fend for themselves again as they had during the annexation crisis. The Germans concentrated their fear and
imagination on the consequences of losing their one remaining ally. The French were convinced that their alliance system might suffer an irreparable blow if they as
much as hesitated in aiding Russia. The British did not
see how they could acquiesce in German control of the
channel ports, let alone in German dominance over
Europe.

None of these fears were groundless, but war was about
as good an answer to them as suicide is to the fear of
death. The war's direct cost, often calculated and described, still fits no category of horror that we are capable
of visualizing. At Verdun alone, perhaps a million Frenchmen and Germans died. How does one picture a million
deaths? How does this small book hold the bloody fields
of France? And bloodied to what end? To the end that
the war would destroy the Austro-Hungarian Empire it
was designed to save, end Russian influence in the Balkans
for years to come, and leave Germany more weak and
lonely than she had ever been before. Nor would it spare
the victors. Without it, Britain might still be the world's
banker and France still the master of an empire extending
from Algeria to Indo-China. "This war," said Franz
Kafka to a friend in 1916, "above all else was caused by
a tremendous lack of imagination."

The lack was understandable. Imagination, in cases
other than Kafka's, more often than not is the extension
of the past into the future, and the past was reassuring.
None of the many crises to which people had been witness
had led to war. Nations had threatened one another, had
dispatched curt notes and large dreadnoughts, but at the
final moment, they had always drawn back, whether over
Fashoda, Morocco, or Bosnia, since none among them
really wanted a general war. Hence, what each side ex-

pected was the customary mixture of public bluster and private good sense. Once more, there would be the walk to the brink; once more, one would, with a suitable show of resistance, permit oneself to be pulled back.

Overconfidence, the alliance system, the press, national antagonisms, militarism—the list still is incomplete unless there is added to it the crucial event that made these and other factors operable. That event was the crime of Gavrilo Princip. Without Sarajevo, Europe might have remained at peace for no one can say how many years to come. 1914 was not 1939. Too much was right with Europe then. The world had weathered (and would again weather) considerably worse periods of crisis without recourse to global conflict. History resists prediction; alliances, attitudes, conditions, constellations of power all change in the normal course of events, often rapidly so. How they had changed between the 1880s and the turn of the century, for instance, and how, with Franz Ferdinand alive, they might have changed once more!

Sarajevo, then, was a major cause of the war, not merely its occasion. Princip killed more than two victims. It was his and Dimitrijević's deed, as well as the errors of fact and judgment that occurred in its aftermath that gave all the various elements of friction their unique opportunity of coalescing. The errors and the pure bad luck, the sheer accidents, from a chauffeur's wrong turn to a German foreign minister's absence honeymooning to a Russian chief of the general staff being new to his office.

No power had any over-all, conscious designs for war in 1914. Nowhere, even in the summer of 1914, was a calculated, advance decision made for global war. Rather, the powers, as a result of Sarajevo, became involved in a series of moves and countermoves—all of them, on the face of it, logical, reasonable, or at least defensible—that stage by stage, step by step, imperceptibly at times, and hardly ever with any true vision of the consequences, placed them in a position from which there was no way back to the negotiating table. Thus, all the trends, events, factors mentioned in these pages, both long-range and immediate, had their bearing on the origins of World War I and were in some manner relevant; thus, too, none of them were. For not one of the factors described was sufficient in itself to cause a war, nor had, in previous years, partly similar combinations of circumstances ended the way Sarajevo did. Perhaps all one can truly say in the end is that World War I was a twentieth century diplomatic crisis gone wrong, the one gamble, or rather series of gambles (of how many in all, before or after?) that did not work out. Such things happen.

Bibliographical Note

Three books form the core of the bibliography of the Causes of the First World War: Sidney B. Fay, *The Origins of the World War* (New York, 1930), Bernadotte E. Schmitt, *The Coming of the War, 1914* (New York, 1930), and Luigi Albertini, *The Origins of the War of 1914* (London, 1952–1957). Some of the details in Fay and Schmitt are now outdated, but on the whole, both books have stood the test of time remarkably well. There has been a Library of Congress card explosion of World War I titles since the appearance of Fay and Schmitt; there have been more primary sources published than even teams of historians could absorb; there has been an entire scholarly periodical that, for the two decades of its existence, devoted itself to nothing but the question of the causes of 1914. Throughout it all, Fay and Schmitt have remained indispensable. Even their biases—Fay tends to absolve the Central Powers of the Versailles war-guilt accusation, while Schmitt holds it to be essentially true—have not really detracted from their worth. Rather, both have defined and documented scholarly positions that all subsequent historians have had to take into account.

The Albertini book is in a somewhat different category. It is a book more likely to be quoted than read. It is a jungle of detail, in which supposition and fact, the germane and the inapposite, the new discovery and the old cliché, the marginal and the essential all dwell side by side, with few discernible efforts on Albertini's part to provide paths or clearings. But if it is a jungle, it also contains treasure. Scarcely a document of any bearing on the topic has escaped the author's scrutiny. (Many of these, of course, were not yet available when Fay and Schmitt appeared.) Hardly an event remains undescribed. In addition, he interviewed or corresponded with many of the participants in the events, asking some shrewd and probing questions and receiving some revealing answers. In sum, then, Albertini's three long, complete, and sometimes exasperating volumes stand as a reference work that any serious student of 1914 will have to consult.

There is a fourth title that should be mentioned with Fay, Schmitt, and Albertini. It is Raymond J. Sontag, *European Diplomatic History, 1871–1932* (New York, 1933). It is not a new book, but it is an inspired one. It is fair, literate, and lucid, a book where nothing is in excess and a model of what diplomatic history can be. Despite its age and the problems this raises in the field of modern diplomatic history, it remains as illuminating as any we have on the period.

There are, in addition to these four, literally thousands of other titles that could be mentioned. Nearly all of the governments involved have released the relevant diplomatic documents, in collections that often go back to the latter part of the nineteenth century. (The principal collecion of French documents alone runs to three series and over thirty volumes, and there are, in this case as in others, several supplementary collections as well.) The only government documents not released so far, those of Serbia, are now finally being edited too and should appear in the late 1960s. Most of the statesmen active at the time have written their memoirs, and there are numerous biographies of both major and minor political figures that in many instances are based on personal or official documents not available elsewhere. There also exists a vast secondary literature on the topic; in quantity of material, World War I is a serious contender to either Napoleon or the American Civil War.

Fortunately, there is no need to attempt the provision of even a skeleton bibliography here—which in its leanest form would still require a good many pages—since several excellent such bibliographies are easily available. Three of the best are the bibliography in volume III of Albertini; the bibliographical essay in Dwight E. Lee, *The Outbreak of the War, Who Was*

Responsible? (New York, 1963), which also provides a fine introduction to the very different interpretations of the war's origins offered by some very distinguished historians; and the listings in the American Historical Association's *Guide to Historical Literature* (New York, 1961). As none of the three, however, take much account of titles published since the late 1950s, it may be useful here to list some of the more important work published since that time. (One further restriction, in the interest of both brevity and utility: the comments that follow will limit themselves to material available in English.)

As for surveys of diplomatic history, the most valuable is that of René Albrecht-Carrié, *A Diplomatic History of Europe Since the Congress of Vienna* (New York, 1958). It is a solid, reliable, and balanced book and preferable, for these qualities, to A. J. P. Taylor's somewhat earlier *The Struggle for Mastery in Europe, 1848–1914* (Oxford, 1954), which ranges from the brilliant to the bizarre. (Thus Taylor, on the Germans and their aims, *circa* 1905: ". . . their real object, not yet formulated in their own minds, was to establish peacefully their predominance over the Continent and thus be free to challenge the British Empire overseas.") However, Taylor manages to be provocative even in his sophistries, and when he is good, he is very very good, and when he is not, he is still seldom dull. There also is a more recent book by Albrecht-Carrié that deserves notice in this connection, *The Meaning of the First World War* (Englewood Cliffs, New Jersey, 1965). It is, as the title indicates, more concerned with consequences than with causes, but it offers, in its introductory sections, the sort of clear and meaningful over-all view confronting pre-1914 Europe that is sometimes in danger of being lost in the more detailed and conventional diplomatic accounts.

Among biographies, two on William II are especially worth citing: Virginia Cowles, *The Kaiser* (New York, 1963) and Michael Balfour, *The Kaiser and His Times* (Boston, 1964). The latest biography of the Chancellor whom William dismissed is by a German journalist, Werner Richter, *Bismarck* (New York, 1965), but probably the best of contemporary writers on

Bismarck is an American, Gordon Craig, whose *From Bismarck
to Adenauer, Aspects of German Statecraft* (Baltimore, 1958)
offers an exceedingly perceptive analysis of Bismarck's diplomatic style. For a view from the other side of the channel, there
is J. A. S. Grenville's solid and sensible *Lord Salisbury and
Foreign Policy: The Close of the Nineteenth Century* (London,
1964).

On the Austro-Hungarian and the wider Southeastern European background of the issues, some excellent work has been
appearing in the past few years. Recommended especially are
L. S. Stavrianos, *The Balkans, 1815–1914* (New York, 1963),
which is based on his larger *The Balkans Since 1453* (New York,
1958), the standard survey in the field; Arthur J. May, *The
Passing of the Hapsburg Monarchy, 1914–1918* (Philadelphia,
1966), and Z. A. B. Zeman, *The Break-Up of the Hapsburg
Empire* (London, 1961), both of which concentrate on a later
period but contain much that is of value for an understanding
of the essential problems of the Danubian monarchy; and the
ambitious but uneven history of that monarchy in the last century of its existence by Edward Crankshaw, *The Fall of the
House of Habsburg* (New York, 1963) .

On a more specialized but crucial topic, it would take extraordinary self-control not to mention Joachim Remak, *Sarajevo, The Story of a Political Murder* (New York, 1959).
Vladimir Dedijer, biographer of Tito and editor designate of
the Serbian documents, has written a book on the assassination
and its antecedents, *The Road to Sarajevo* (New York, 1966)
which is based on a wide variety of sources and is particularly
good in its description of the Bosnian background. Worth
noting, too, is an article by Dedijer, evaluating some new material on the plot, "Sarajevo Fifty Years After" in *Foreign
Affairs,* XLII (July, 1964) , 569–584. Another, rather rambling
contribution to the field, Dennison I. Rusinow, "Assassination
at Sarajevo: The Fiftieth Anniversary," *American Universities
Field Staff Report Service* (Southeast Europe Series), XI, 779–
796, contains some interesting comments on the current Yugo-
slav attitude toward the events of June 28, which continues to
fluctuate between embarrassment and admiration.

The crisis that followed Sarajevo is beautifully summed up in a pamphlet written by Bernadotte Schmitt for the British Historical Association, *The Origins of the First World War* (London, 1958), and its final phase is described in a well written and well documented book by a British journalist, George Malcolm Thomson, *The Twelve Days, 24 July to 4 August 1914* (New York, 1964). Bernadotte Schmitt also has written a brief essay on the importance of the press as well as on the limits of that importance—a topic to which relatively little has been contributed since the appearance of Oron J. Hale's *Publicity and Diplomacy* in 1940—"The Relation of Public Opinion and Foreign Affairs before and during the First World War," in *Studies in Diplomatic History and Historiography in Honor of G. P. Gooch, C. H.*, ed. by A. D. Sarkissian, (London, 1961) .

For the larger, underlying causes of the war, two recent titles are especially worth noting, one German, the other American. The former is Fritz Fischer, *Griff nach der Weltmacht* (3d. ed., Düsseldorf, 1964), of which W. W. Norton should have brought out an American edition by the time this sees print. Its primary emphasis is on Germany's war aims, but the introductory sections on the causes of the war—in which Fischer sees Germany as culpable indeed—have caused more discussion than any other book on the period that has appeared within a generation. Fischer's thesis at best is an arguable one. What he has done, however (the words are Theodor Mommsen's, recalled by Fritz Stern of Columbia during one of the many Fischer debates) has been "to strike the blow that creates a thousand new connections." Another book by the same author, devoted entirely to the origins of the war, is in preparation. The American title is Laurence Lafore's *The Long Fuse, An Interpretation of the Origins of World War I* (Philadelphia, 1965). Unlike Fischer's book, it is based on a reinterpretation of the literature on the war's origins rather than on a study of the primary sources; on the other hand, its conclusions are rather more tenable. It is written with great elegance and style, and it sensibly focuses on the Southeastern European setting of the War. Lafore sees Fay and Schmitt as having been unduly preoccupied with the war-guilt question and with the role of Ger-

many, and therefore as having blocked from view what should
have been obvious, that without the quarrel between Austria
and Serbia, there would have been no World War in 1914.
The point is a good one, and Lafore provides an excellent
balance to the accounts with which he takes issue.

Two other titles, also American, may complete this list. One
is Herman Kahn's *On Thermonuclear War* (Princeton, 1961),
which contains some sharp and fresh comments on how the
details of military planning in 1914 worked to deprive the
statesmen of their true freedom of action. The other is George
Kennan's, "The Price We Paid for War," *The Atlantic* CCXIV,
50–54 (October 1964), where the distinguished diplomat and
historian offers some thoughtful and stimulating reflections on
the war's causes as well as costs.

A special note of appreciation, finally, is owed to a number
of authors and publishers who have graciously permitted the
quotation of copyrighted material cited in this volume. They
are Sidney B. Fay, *The Origins of the World War*, The Macmillan Company; Gustav Janouch, *Gespräche mit Kafka*, S.
Fischer Verlag; Herman Kahn, *On Thermonuclear War*, Princeton University Press; Theodore Roethke, "The Victorians," in
Poetry in Crystal, Steuben Glass; Raymond J. Sontag, *European Diplomatic History, 1871–1932*, Appleton-Century-Crofts;
and A. J. P. Taylor, *The Struggle for Mastery in Europe, 1848–
1914*, Oxford University Press; as well as *The Atlantic Monthly*,
for the George Kennan quotations, and *Der Monat*, for those
by Golo Mann and Johannes Urzidil. It was the latter magazine,
too, that prefaced a series of articles on 1914 with a Bismarck
sentence that, as far as the copyright laws are concerned, is
now in the public domain: "It is not the task of politics to
avenge what has happened, but to prevent its recurrence."

Index